"These eleven stories of courage in the face of adversity are a true inspiration. Each woman tells of her struggle against two overpowering forces in her life: the paralyzing effects of self-doubt, and the seemingly insurmountable odds of beating the hand that life dealt her. With unflinching honesty and in frequently heartbreaking detail, the women recount their journeys through spousal abuse, financial obstacles, crippling illnesses, humiliating setbacks, and family tragedies. Their trials and ultimate triumphs will inspire and motivate you as you read their words and rejoice in their achievements."

—Robin Ann Reed
Soul coach and energy healer
Spring Green, WI

"The power of story is the way it connects us - not only with each other but with ourselves. But this book goes way beyond that. Not only do these stories create connection, they help us better understand ourselves and others - courtesy of the Endotype Formula profiles they highlight. That is the real gift of this book. These stories give us permission to be the unique human beings we are designed to be."

—Teresa Romain
President, Access Abundance Inc.
Wisconsin Dells, WI

An Anthology: Beth Kille, Mindy Wilson, Michelle Saunders, Wendy Herrmann, Lisa Nelson, Elaine Turso, Keely Crook, Abbie Lorene, & Cindy Strom

Printed in the United States of America

Published by Author Academy Elite

P.O. Box 43, Powell, OH 43035

Laura Hulleman S6185 Bluff Rd, Merrimac WI 53561 info@endotype.com www.endotype.com

Angela Witczak 326 Badger Drive Baraboo WI 53913 choosetoday366@gmail.com www.choosetoday366.com

Paperback: 978-1-64746-944-3

Hardback: 978-1-64746-945-0

E-book: 978-1-64746-946-7

(LCCN): 2021921481

My Walk, My Way: Women Who Changed Their Lives One Step At A Time

An Anthology

Compiled by Laura Hulleman and Angela Witczak

Laura's Dedication

I am truly honored be able to help tell the stories contained here in this book. I would first like to dedicate this work to the women authors who shared their vulnerability, heartaches, and lessons in their chapters. Because you were willing to dive deeply into your feelings, I am able to help people understand their Endotype Formula better. You will never know the lives that you are changing by sharing your stories.

Next I want to thank my collaborator, conspirator and bestie Angela. Happy 10 year friendiversary! I can't think of a better way to celebrate than to make friends with a bunch of other women and empower them to speak their truth. I appreciate you always being a willing test case for the Endotype Formula and allowing me to send you 10 minute voice messages when I just need to talk something out. "Saved that one."

I also want to thank the myriad of men and women who have supported and poured into me over the years. Coaches, accountability partners, gym ladies, fellow Dots, loyal friends and amazing (crazy) family. I dare not mention names for fear I would miss one. I could not be the person that I am now without each amazing person I have met along my walk. You fill my heart and make me shine.

I could never end this without mentioning the two greatest lights in my life, Jesse and Logan Hulleman. Every day you make me smile, laugh, and warm my soul with your genuine awesomeness. That totally makes up for the few times you make me want to pull my hair out. You continue to impress me by simply being who you are. I am beyond grateful that I have gotten to by your parent. Stay weird.

Angela's Dedication

I had just released my first book, when I was talking to my best friend about this problem. The problem that truly haunts all of us. The ugly comparison issue so many of us seem to struggle with. "So what if WE write the book?" she said. And that is how My Walk, My Way was formed.

Laura, my dear best friend, my life has never been the same since I walked into your gym 11 years ago, and I couldn't be more proud. These words and lessons we have learned over the years, along with the stories from our friends, will change the lives of others.

I would not have wanted to forge this path with anyone else but you.

For my husband, Edward, thank you for climbing every mountain, and forging every valley with me. Our life has been an adventure to the fullest extreme and I am glad you have been by my side through it all. Many thanks to my children, who have taught me patience beyond measure, and how to never give up.

And for you, dear reader, these stories are for you. May you find comfort and permission to know that while your journey is your own, you are never alone. There will always be women here beside you.

I love you. I believe in you. Be well.

Table of Contents

Introduction

Hello. I'm Laura Hulleman, and I'm Angela Witczak. We are the collaborators and collectors of this book. With nine other authors, we contributed to the creation of *My Walk, My Way.* This book has been written to counter a problem we have experienced most of our lives. This problem stops women from reaching out and makes the ones who do reach out for more feel like they are being selfish. This problem creates catty, cutthroat gossip that can grow like a deadly infection in women's relationships. The problem is comparison.

From the time we are very young we begin to be compared to others. At school, we are compared to other students. At home, we are compared to our siblings. On our teams, we are scored and compared to other participants. Being good little girls (and boys) we begin to compare ourselves to our peers. We compare our bodies, grades, friends, hair, family, fashion, everything.

This does not stop as we age. In our adult years, we compare our education, religion, pants size, children, career, trauma, possessions, and relationships to those of others. We look on social media to compare our everyday lives to someone else's highlights reel. It leads to mom-shaming, slut-shaming, and body policing. I am not talking about men doing this to women. I am talking about we women doing this to each other. You, consciously or not, rank yourself as better than or less than many of the people in your life. You have been raised to do this, and yet there is a high price to pay for it. This culture assaults our confidence, our self-love, our personal identity, and our joy.

We all know the solution is to do life on our terms, and yet our learned behavior and culture of comparison are hard to break away from. This book is made to be an inspirational exercise in ending comparison.

Life's Journey

For ages books, songs, poetry, and movies have compared life to a road, path, or journey. Our lives are a walk we take and each very different. When I am invited to walk with someone, I always require clarification. Are we taking a stroll through town, or are we climbing the 900-foot ascent of Devil's Lake State Park? Will we be trekking through swampy wetlands, or is this the morning 5K that my friend Angela loves so much? When I understand what type of walk I will be on, I can evaluate if I am physically prepared for that type of undertaking.

However, in life, we do not always get to choose our walk. Through our journey, there will be trauma, unexpected decisions, or we may find ourselves off our path. These are just the twists in the road, potholes or rocks in our path, and uphill climbs. They are not permanent unless we do nothing to change them. Each step we take can and will be our next transformation.

In this book, our authors share with you the challenges common (and some not so common) to us all. These authors have opened themselves up in a vulnerable and beautiful way to show us how they have intentionally changed their lives one step at a time.

Life is not about hanging our heads down and just plowing our way through life. No, each day, we have choices that we make on our road of life. Depending on what we choose to do will affect the direction it takes. We hope these amazing stories inspire you to take on your life in a new way. You have options in your journey. It's time to explore them.

Doing it Your Way

Over the years, we have looked to books for inspiration, advice, and answers to many of life's challenges. Both of us (Angela and Laura) have fallen into a *huge pitfall* while doing this. Books hold a wealth of knowledge, inspiration, experiences, and answers. However, when reading the work of Brené Brown, Mel Robbins, Shonda Rhimes, Rachel Hollis, or even Oprah Winfrey, we have fallen under the spell of the guru. We found ourselves thinking, "So, all I have to do is be more like her. She has her life altogether. If I am more like her, *then* my life will be better." Or perhaps yours sounds more like, "I'll never succeed *because* I am not as (bold, smart, kind, powerful) as this author."

These authors wrote some amazing books. But, comparing ourselves to our favorite authors didn't serve us, AND was holding us back. There is nothing wrong when we connected with their circumstance and situation. There is nothing wrong with adding their advice and tips to our mental or emotional pack for our life journey. The problem arises when we feel like we have to be more like them to fix ourselves. Oh, my sweet friend, trust me when I say, you are not broken. I am not broken. **We are NOT broken.**

Our belief that we are broken comes from our old nemesis, comparison. In this book, we decided to intentionally challenge your default desire to compare. We collected stories from 11 different women. We are born in different places, with different educations, career paths, cultures, etc.

However, each author is also fundamentally different in their thinking, motivation, gifts, and cravings. I know this for a fact because we intentionally chose women from different Endotypes.™

I (Laura) have spent the last six years researching and recognizing the patterns that created the Endotype Formula™, the most comprehensive and advanced personality assessment available at this time. This incredible system explains how people are designed. What I learned through this is that I cannot be like Brené, Mel, Shonda, Rachel, or Oprah. All of these amazing women have an Endotype different from mine. When writing their books, they are explaining what worked for them. They are writing and living through their perspective, their Endotype Formula. Because of this, their advice on parenting, dieting, marriage, business, and personal growth may not work for me at all. And, it is unrealistic to believe I can *be like them* if I follow said advice.

We created this book so you can stop comparing yourself to others. Here you can learn about your design: how you work, what you are great at, and how at times your design may cause you to stumble. Inside, you will find stories highlighting the challenges women face in life, from career and family to our bodies and abuse. (Trigger warning: sexuality, as well as emotional and physical abuse and foul language are discussed in this book). Our deep desire is for you to connect with these women, draw inspiration from their stories, but not to compare yourselves with them. To help you do this, we are inviting you to learn what Endotype you are.

Our Mission

Before you begin to read this book, we invite you to take the Endotype Formula quiz at www.mywalkmyway.com. There you will see a link to take the quick five questions quiz and determine your Endotype. You will be able to see a description of your Endotype and have that profile emailed to you. As you start reading, you will see the Endotype of each author noted.

Knowing these Endotypes serves *three purposes*. First, as you read an author with the same, or similar, Endotype as yourself, see if you can understand the choices she made. Look for ways to relate. Do you share similar doubts or struggles? Can you see how some of their strengths are also your strengths? Don't attempt to use this as a strict how-to.

Second, as you read the stories of different Endotypes, you have an opportunity to practice reducing comparison. Because our default mode is "better than" or "worse than", we are quick to judge the actions of others. This may lead to us thinking, "Why would they ever do that?" Or perhaps, "I am so dumb. I never would have thought about doing that." That is our rotten comparison habit creeping up. Instead, as you read, seek to understand and empathize with the author. You cannot place yourself in their shoes, so don't try. You can honor the walk they have taken, and learn about their Endotype. Look for ways you can draw inspiration from their vulnerability and courage.

Our third purpose is for you to try and get a peek inside the minds of people you meet in your day-to-day lives. Have your partners, spouses, co-workers, or friends take the Endotype Formula quiz. When you know their Endotype, you can re-read their chapter. Seek to understand their strengths, inner motivators, and cravings that they may find difficult to share with you. Understanding others facilitates connection over comparison.

"I can't find an author with the same Endotype as me."

There are a total of sixteen Endotypes. In this book we have authors from ten of those. You may take the Endotype Formula quiz and find we do not have an author with the exact same Endotype title as you (Example: Lost Pancreas Captain). For each Endotype there are several that have a similar design. On page 145 of this book, you will find the Endotype Q & A section. There we have created four groups of Endotypes that are similar. If we do not have an author with the same Endotype as you, or you would like to see who you are like or different from, please consult that chart.

We are grateful for the opportunity to share these stories with you. Notice in each story, the author made a monumental shift in their lives. However, it was not just one change. It would be absurd to imagine ourselves climbing a mountain without practice. These women made not just one single change, but a series of small life shifts and choices. Please believe that through small steps you too can overcome any challenges in your walk, your way.

No matter your age, you are still on the journey. Our walk is not done until we are being placed into the ground. Each day you get to choose. Will you continue walking as you have been told you should by others, or will you let the critical voice of comparison shame you into choices? Oh, my friends, you are capable of all that you have done, and so much more!

We hope you will finish this book by taking on the challenge of *My Walk, My Way!*

Sincerely,

Laura Hulleman and Angela Witczak

Chapter 1
Why Haven't You Made It Yet?

By Beth Kille
Angry Thymus Visionary

When he said, "Wow! I can't believe you haven't *made it in music,*" what I heard was, "Hey, maybe if you worked harder and got your shit together, you'd be a totally famous bazillionaire!" Have any of you ever had an experience like that?

It was the Fall of 2009, and I was one year out from quitting my day job and had just finished an intimate house concert in a Chicago suburb. I was basking in the electric, addictive buzz of having laughed, cried, and connected with the audience. A friendly gentleman soon approached me with that statement. I knew it was meant as a compliment, but that day, it made my fragile heart sink.

When I quit my day job to pursue a career in music in 2008, I thought I'd better do something to prove to society that I hadn't lost my mind. I'd spent seven years at the University of Wisconsin-Madison, earned my master's degree in Physical Therapy, and racked up some impressive grad school debt *en route* to what many considered an excellent, secure, and well-paying career. I enjoyed the work and was fascinated by the human body. I also loved my colleagues and connecting with my patients, frequently literally helping them get back on their feet. It was challenging, and it felt like I was contributing to society.

However, I was also a lifelong musician and a right-brained creative spirit. I grew up surrounded by music. There was a nicked-up, mahogany-colored upright piano in the cozy house on Williams Street in Marinette, WI, where I grew up. In his youth, my dad (Bob) played accordion in a polka band. On the weekends, he and I would sit at the piano, my feet not touching the ground, and he'd let me be his "left hand" while we played Boogie-woogie songs.

My mom (Sue) was a singer, actor, and poet who bought vinyl records (the first iteration of vinyl) and encouraged my sister and me to dance around the living room, belting out Cyndi Lauper tunes into our hairbrushes. My parents' creative endeavors weren't their livelihoods. They owned and operated Bob's Tire and Auto Service Center in our small town. My dad, by nature, was a hardworking businessman, but keeping the books for a vehicle repair shop was not my mom's passion.

Mom was alive on the stage. I vividly remember her starring in the roles of Anna in *The King and I* and Marian in *The Music Man*. My dad would drive my sister and me to the Theater on the Bay to watch her. I can still feel the soft red velvet of the theater seats and the thrill I felt when the lights dimmed, and the curtain rose. My hair would stand up on the back of my neck when the voices of the cast would harmonize. It was amazing to see her in this light.

Occasionally, her actor friends would show up at the house, or I'd get to join the cast party after a show. I didn't know it then, but these experiences let me internalize that there was no great divide between the people on stage and me. They weren't larger than life. They were just everyday folks who would come over, high-five me, and have a beer and cigarette in the kitchen. In my world, performance was open to anyone.

The ubiquity of music in my early years set me ahead of the pack when it came time to join the middle school band. I "matched" with a clarinet, and I took to it like the ultimate band nerd. I don't ever remember my parents forcing me to practice. I just did it. It got me in the flow. I felt my classmates rolling their eyes at me, thinking, *What a brown-noser!* But I wasn't doing this to show anyone up.

When I attended summer Band Camp, I found my freaking people. I didn't have to feel like a goodie two-shoes. The music was just inside me, and it had to come out. These band campers completely understood that. Finding this community was precisely what I needed to embrace my inner song.

My mother also instilled in me a love of words. To Mom, language was a playground. She would recite silly poems like "Spring has sprung, the grass is riz. I wonder where the flowers is!" There were even made-up terms, like a "Gilby," which was a term her family used for a goofy smile in a picture. She read to my sister and me every night when we were little. We'd sit on either side of her on our black-and-white tweed sofa while she brought Judy Blume stories to life and made Shel Silverstein poems sing. Mother inspired me to write my poems, many of which she still keeps in a scrapbook. I remember her holding meetings at our house with fellow poets, reading their works to each other. She lived what she preached by surrounding herself with creative people as just a way of life. Mom thrived with actors and poets. I thrived with the band and orchestra kids.

Mom may have given me the words, but I think Dad gave me the music. I inherited a beautiful affliction from my father. There is always music playing in his head. It's like a personal radio tower embedded in his skull. When my mom catches him drumming the steering wheel in a silent car, she'll ask, "So, what's playing on WBOB today?"

I have my own non-stop music stream. It can wake me up from a dead sleep. Sometimes it's an earworm by one of my favorite artists where the lyrics won't stop rolling in my head. (Embarrassingly, I can still sing along word for word to almost any Top-40 pop song from the '80s.) It is a new song that falls out of the ether into my brain more often.

When I was going into 7th grade, I took summer group band lessons. One week, our band instructor gave us a composition assignment. We had to write a few bars of an original song and be prepared to play it the next lesson. I was jazzed! I was excited to write one of these bad boys down and play it on my clarinet.

I vividly recall a couple of my classmates, bright ones even, being utterly befuddled by this composition assignment. This puzzled me. This was the first time I realized not everyone had neurons that hum, strum, sing, and drum. I was weird.

Throughout high school, I continued to play music and geek out in my English classes. Still, my fascination with human behavior pulled me toward wanting to pursue a career in Psychology. I envisioned myself as a much kinder Lucy from *Peanuts* comic strip, dispensing advice and solving the world's woes.

My band director gently nudged me to continue to pursue music, but I thought it wasn't practical. You can't make a living making music, right? I mean, who does that? Nobody in my small town made a living as an artist—nobody. Art is a hobby.

When I got to the University of Wisconsin-Madison in autumn of 1992, I auditioned for the UW Marching Band. While pursuing my psychology degree, I had the honor of marching beside 250 of the most badass band nerds in the history of band nerds. I was in my happy place with these people. I even fell in love with and married one of the flugelhorn players. I spent five happy years under the direction of the infamous Michael Leckrone. I served as the drum major for two years, twirling a baton and encouraging my bandmates to push through the often-grueling heat, cold, dust, mud, rain, sprained ankles, bloody lips, and *harness hickeys*. (Ask someone who marched with a snare drum to tell you about this one.)

In my final year of undergrad, it was time to start applying to graduate programs in psychology, but I had a horrible realization. I was a person completely unable to hold still. How the hell could I sit behind a desk and listen to people talk? After attending some volunteer opportunities with support groups, I discovered that hearing about people's troubles and the abuses they had suffered made me want to hunt down bad guys and beat them up—two strikes against my dream of being *Nice Lucy*. I had to switch gears.

A former roommate was completing her degree in Occupational Therapy and said I should investigate Physical Therapy. So, I did. And I dug it. There was no sitting still with this profession. And most of the time, people hurt themselves unintentionally, so I didn't feel the need to assault any perpetrators. I fell into this new track. Looking back on it, I realize it was a different way to appease my desire to help people improve their lives. Instead of brain rehab, I'd be doing bodywork.

I spent my days at grad school in biker shorts and a sports bra, poking and prodding classmates amid vast piles of textbooks and three-ring binders. I fell into the routine of study, go to class, study, and then when you are tired of that, you study and go to class. There wasn't time for much else. So it wasn't surprising that I had a small minor breakdown in December of my first year of Physical Therapy school.

One of my classmates invited me to her church's Christmas concert. I needed a break from the grind and thought it would cheer me up to see some cute kiddos dressed as angels singing about Jesus. Instead, what I found was a well-oiled machine of incredible musicians, singing and playing the most gorgeous music I'd ever heard. I sat in the back of that church with tears streaming down my face. I figured it was just fatigue or PMS until I realized that I had gone almost a year without making music.

In grad school, I was surrounded by academics. I loved these people, but they weren't MY community. It was the first time in my life I had no creative outlet. And I was pretty sure I was going to die. I went to my PT school advisor and bawled. I was losing it! Fortunately, she spoke to me in soothing tones and looked at me with empathetic eyes. As a fellow creative spirit and a novice guitarist, she suggested picking up a new instrument. Her idea resonated, so I found a super-cheap acoustic guitar and started plucking.

This was back before the days of YouTube, so I bought *Guitar Playing for Dummies,* and I dove in. I didn't devote a ton of time to it until I finished the didactic portion of my PT studies, but once I was in the clinic full time as an intern, I was able to carve out some time after work to come home at night and noodle. I knew I wanted to do more than play. Even though I didn't consider myself a singer, I immediately combined my strumming with my voice. It seemed like the perfect way to meld my passion for music and words.

I wasn't planning on just singing songs from the radio either; I would write my OWN stuff! Clueless about where to start, I just learned a few chords and wrote a few ideas down, only figuring it would just be something fun to do when I wasn't helping people rehab their busted knees and slipped discs.

When I landed my first real job as a PT, one of my patients was a friendly fellow named Andy who hurt his shoulder lugging around his guitar amp. Over the weeks of treatment, I mentioned that I was a novice guitarist and was messing around with songwriting. He immediately invited me to join his songwriting group, but my initial reaction was, "Oh no, I only play quietly in my room where no one hears me." It's also weird being a care provider and seeing your patients outside that setting, so I declined. A few months after I discharged him from care, though, he called and invited me again. This time I figured I had nothing to lose.

I walked into a cramped rehearsal room with a handful of creative souls who were all around ten years my senior. I had never sung or played my guitar in front of anyone besides my husband before. I felt nervous, but it also felt right. I've never been particularly averse to standing up and making an ass of myself, and these folks showered me with kind words and bright smiles. They taught me tricks and techniques and brought it all down to a level that made sense.

This writing group slowly evolved into a band called Watershed, with five different songwriters. We played a handful of small gigs over a couple of years. I loved standing on stage before an attentive audience. I had also been bitten hard by a songwriting bug and started to amass more songs than a band with five different lead singers could accommodate. So I eventually branched off to form my band called Clear Blue Betty. We were weekend warriors, playing around the state and gaining some momentum.

After a few years of working full-time as a PT and part-time as a musician, I started to feel like I was losing it again. I had hoped that the weekend bar gigs and summer festivals might quiet the radio station in my head, but it had quite the opposite effect. During my shifts, I would run back into my office between treating a lady with a total knee replacement and a dude with a rotator cuff repair and jot down lyrics on scrap paper.

I'd even call my answering machine on my lunch break and sing melodies that popped into my head so I wouldn't forget them. (This was before the days of fancy cell phones with recording apps.) I eventually decided to cut my hours to half-time to devote more time to music.

In 2008, my husband was unexpectedly invited to do a year of job training in Houston, Texas. I decided it was a sign; time to take the plunge and kiss my day job goodbye. It wasn't without a ton of sleepless nights. My intuition was telling me that I had to dive in thoroughly to make it in music, but my ego worried about the whispering that might happen behind my back.

Saying goodbye to my PT colleagues was gut-wrenching. We all gathered in the gym over an impromptu lunch meeting that my supervisor called to break the news. Many of them had shocked faces as I cried, telling them I was leaving and planned to pursue a new career in music. I will never forget how one of my dearest coworkers, who was so passionate about my creative life, just nodded and smiled at me with her bright blue eyes. She was silently saying, "You go, girl!"

Moving to a city a thousand miles away and taking up a "new" job made my heart race for many reasons. Terrifying? Yes. Exhilarating? Absolutely. Overwhelming? Definitely. Despite these overlapping emotions, I knew I would regret it for the rest of my life if I didn't at least try. The first thing I did was to look for my "community."

Living in the music-friendly state of Texas made it easy to get serious about the craft and business of songwriting. I joined a local writer's group that had its main headquarters in the almighty music Mecca of Nashville. One of the first people I met was the rockin' fairy godmother of the Houston music scene, Connie Mims. Connie took me under her wing, introduced me to many writers, wrote with me, and put me on stage to perform. She also roped me in to teach a crash course in songwriting for this Grammy Career Day, attended by high schoolers from the Houston area. I was utterly green to teaching, but she wisely partnered me with a talented and kindhearted local Latin music guru named Walter.

Students bounced into our small, white-tiled classroom and ate up our lessons like ravenous wolves. One exercise involved giving them mundane objects, like pieces of jewelry or paper clips, to spark their imagination for lyrics. My jaw hit the ground! I was jumping up and down and pumping my fists in the air in excitement when I heard what these young and unfiltered minds could create. After we had wrapped up, I ran to my car and immediately dialed my mother to tell her how thrilling it was to help these kids express their creativity.

While stationed in Houston, I also made a point of frequenting Nashville. There were tons of excellent professionals there willing to help you tweak a lyric or suggest a new chord progression. It was here that I learned that there were songwriters who were simply that. Songwriters. They weren't standing on stages anywhere; they penned the tunes for folks like Carrie Underwood and Blake Shelton. And they could make a shit ton of money doing it. I also gleaned that as a 34-year-old woman, I was a dinosaur in the eyes of the music industry, so any dream I harbored of becoming a superstar myself was supposedly foolhardy.

I knew in my heart that performing my songs was my passion, but who the hell did I think I was? How could some "old" lady who didn't even have a music degree, who was kind of a hack on the guitar and only an adequate singer think she could become the next big thing? And if I didn't earn at least as much money making music as I did with my day job, was I just living off my husband's money and shirking adult responsibilities? Well, then, I would just have to become the next big thing in the songwriting world.

I started trying to write for other people. Slight problem with that approach? It wasn't where my skills or passion lay. I was following my ego, wanting to prove myself by making money, and was completely ignoring my heart.

I always prided myself on my work ethic. However, the occasional question of "So now that you're not working anymore, what do you do with all your time?" from a curious friend in the 9-to-5 world stung like a slap in the face. If people couldn't see that my life was actually more challenging now that I didn't walk into a building where someone handed me my schedule and sent me a paycheck every two weeks, well, I would just show them how busy I could be.

In 2009, my husband's Texas training ended, and we returned to Madison, WI. I was on a mission. I would do ALL the things, so I would never have anyone question my worth again. For the next five years, I played hundreds of shows. I was a member of four different bands, made trips to Nashville to pitch songs to publishers, ran an open mic, and started a songwriting club at a local high school. I also taught songwriting workshops, organized a quarterly showcase highlighting women singers, became the Executive Producer of a Grammy-style local awards show, and started an annual Americana music festival.

I released several albums, opened my home studio to record and produce albums for other artists, crafted handmade jewelry from my guitar strings, and co-founded a summer day camp called Girls Rock Camp Madison. Oh, and I had a baby. No one was asking m, "What do you do now that you're not working?" anymore. I had a handful of people who called me "the hardest working woman in showbiz," but I was often still lying awake at night, trying to figure it all out.

Looking back on that, part of me wants to go back and grab my younger self by the shoulders and exclaim, "What the actual f@ck, Beth?" But then there's the realistic, older-and-wiser version of me that knows that I learn by doing. Some of these roads are ones I still happily travel. And while others led to brick walls, they helped me uncover my authentic self, find my community, and land on my definition of success.

The Grammy Day teaching experience in Houston was one of the things that inspired me to co-found Girls Rock Camp (GRC) Madison. GRC is a one-week day camp where campers aged eight to 18 come to learn an instrument, write a song, and rock out in front of hundreds of screaming fans at an end-of-camp showcase.

We held our first camp in 2010 in an unoccupied former music store with 32 campers and a handful of staff. The satirical mantra from my days marching in front of the UW-Madison marching band as the drum major, "Follow me! I have no idea where I'm going!" rang so true to me in this situation. We had a great crew of competent folks on the ship, but it was still scary steering us into uncharted waters. Fortunately, the camp went exceptionally well, and the experience hooked me like an addict.

Two years after starting up the camp, I made one of my trips to Nashville. On that particular trip, I had the stunning realization that a town crawling in starving songwriters all trying to land the next hit single was not my happy place. Throughout my many visits to that town, I met many talented, kind, and beautiful souls and started to make some inroads. But on that last trip, I mostly felt like puking.

Every meeting I had sitting across from a supposed VIP made my skin crawl. At one particular luncheon, a well-intentioned friend was singing my praises to a bigwig who was positioned to help me make "my huge break." All I could think was, "I have to get out of here." Songs are business on the infamous "Music Row," but it suddenly became clear to me; that was NOT why I was into music. I realized that I had way more in common with the eight to eighteen-year-olds who attended Girls Rock Camp Madison. They came to this outrageous summer experience to try something untamed, jam with friends, and write from the heart so they could take the stage in front of people who loved and supported them.

This moment was akin to the Christmas concert meltdown in grad school that led to my "Guitar Playing for Dummies." And that dramatic come-to -Jesus moment with my coworkers as I quit my day job. It was a breakdown of sorts, but this time I was clear-headed and dry-eyed. The radio station in my head stopped playing static and clicked onto my f#@king station.

Of all the musical endeavors I dabbled in, Girls Rock Camp is the one thing that I know for sure is my life's work. It's where I am surrounded by *my people,* and I get to exercise my gifts to inspire people to reach higher, dig deeper, and share their voices. It's the thing that, if I die tomorrow and this is all I ever helped to create, I'll have died happy. I want it etched into my tombstone. When people ask the hypothetical question, "If you had unlimited time, money, and resources, what would you do?" the answer I give is, "I would build a bigger, better, more ass-kicking Girls Rock Camp."

I also know, beyond a doubt, that I love standing on stage and performing my tunes. When the pandemic shut down all stages in 2020, I missed the interaction with the audience like a desert misses the rain. In the hundreds of shows I've played around the Midwest, I've come to realize that the fans I've collected "get" the songs I sing, and they dig my imperfect voice because I passionately sing my truth. My bandmates and friends in the Madison songwriting community know that we aren't competing to be the next big thing in the music industry. We are co-creating and inspiring each other.

My authentic self wants to pull out the best in other people. It's not as a psychologist or physical therapist, though; it is a performer and songwriting instructor who helps run a rock camp and encourages fellow artists to find their unique voice, bringing it to life through song. And my definition of success isn't tied to fame or money. It is linked to the beautiful interconnectedness that is derived through the sharing of an artist's gift.

Holy shit. It turns out I have made it.

So I ask you now, dear reader, to contemplate these questions:

Where is your community?

What does your authentic voice want to sing?

What is your definition of success?

Is it possible you've already made it, but allowing society/family/ego to dictate what success looks like is holding you back from acknowledging your accomplishment?

Where are your people, and how can you surround yourself with your people so you can uplift one another?

And, most importantly, how will you share your light with others?

When you find your true passion, embrace it. The light you radiate will outshine the shadows of doubt, and grace those who surround you.

WILD AND RADIANT LIGHT

B Kille (c) 2020

I have been chasing your approval

Basing my whole self-worth

on what you see in me

I have been bracing for an earful

of all the hurtful words

and what you really think.

The lies I tell myself

and the judgment I project...

It's liberating and terrifying

to know it's in my head

It's only in my head

(Chorus)

I can be the star that shines tonight

I will find the love to make it right

I will be the source of a wild and radiant light

a wild and radiant light

I have been living in a dark space

and taking my energy

from a scared and lonely child

She is surviving deep inside me

waiting patiently

for me to reconcile

the power that I hold

with the fear that keeps me low

It's liberating and terrifying to see where I can go

to see where I can go

repeat chorus

With radical compassion

and unrelenting love

With ruthless with forgiveness

I will rise above; I will rise above

repeat chorus

      I heard the statement, "I can't believe you never *made it*" again in the Spring of 2021, and it didn't even faze me. Because, you see, even though I'm not a mega-wealthy international household name, I know with all my heart that I have made it, just on my terms. There have been a few breakdowns along the way, but each led me to a breakthrough. And now, I build community through performance, and I create opportunities for others to sing their tunes. And there is nothing I would rather do.

Chapter 2:

A Masterpiece in the End

by Mindy Wilson

Overwhelmed Thymus Harmonizer

Hot, wet face—I cannot control the tears, my body still shaking from pleading, "Please give me my child back!" grabbing fiercely with a mother's grip for my youngest son, to no avail. The intense red pain hit my heart as his words, "I will call the cops on you and take your children away," pierced my soul. I wasn't winning the battle this time as I reluctantly walked out of the house to get my daughter to her chiropractic appointment. The pressing thought, "Why can't I control the tears like I always do in public?"

This is the chiropractor's office, I have been taking my oldest child for years and today is her appointment, her time! The echo of my boys laughing, playing with Lego bricks, and my oldest sitting on the adjustment table patiently waiting.

As I sat in the room with the calming music and deep blue aroma scent filling the space, my mind was engulfing blackness. Part of me wanted my friend, Dr. Meacham, to see me silently screaming for help so I could finally be free from the cage. But the other part wanted to keep pretending everything was fine and shrink down. Dr. Meacham walked in and gave me a quick, firm handshake while smiling and directed his attention towards my daughter, saying, "I'm so glad to see you today. Shall we get started?" With a glance at me before starting the adjustment for my daughter, he, as always, noticed the tears pouring from my eyes. He bent down in front of me, and staring into my eyes as no one has ever done before, asked, "Mindy, do you trust me?" That question seemed to be like a bright orange color poking through my black for a split second. He saw me! He saw me!

Have you ever visited an art gallery and been drawn to the beauty of a painting from afar but been pulled closer to the canvas to see all the colors smear together? From a distance, the colors on the canvas make a masterpiece. However, the closer you look, there are so many shades of colors that glide together to create the masterpiece into what it is; it's mind-blowing.

My canvas was filled with grays, dark browns, reds, and indigo. I was good at observing and watching the world around me, but in doing that, I was also handing the paintbrush over to everyone else. I didn't think I could add to my own masterpiece. I didn't feel intelligent, worthy, or good enough. I was always trying to please others, so I handed them the brush.

What I wished and longed for was somewhere I could say I truly belonged. I wanted my canvas to be filled with more yellow, blue, and ivory where I had a large group of friends; self-doubt and internal bondage didn't overtake the painting. I went through the daily routine of school, attending church, and the activities while being in the world; however, I always felt the constant pull of imposter syndrome. It felt confusing and like a heavy weight when I would get a school task, or put myself out there just a little bit, because what would immediately follow would be feelings of anxiety, self-doubt, and worry.

I was taken back to a time when I felt alone and out of place. I sat on the high school bathroom floor, eating my comfort food—my dark brown chocolate and light brown peanut butter cups—so dark brown and so comforting. Maybe it was so comfortable because that's how my whole life felt—just dark brown. It was lunch hour. I could imagine tables and tables filled with all the different groups.

Knowing I did not have a *group* to go eat lunch with, sadness filled my soul, and yet, a sense of calm because, you see, I had a plan! I would just try and do one more thing differently the next day to fit in. I would continue to be *a good student*, graduate high school, and then I would find my *group*.

Well, graduation day had come and gone, and I was determined to splash some yellow and orange onto my canvas. Falling forward into college and studying in my hometown and working, this was my safe world. I knew how it worked and what I had to do to accomplish the task. I immersed myself in the routine for about a year until an opportunity arose, and I could not say no! I was offered room and board from an uncle in Utah.

An adventure of a lifetime and a change of scenery awaited me. My heart raced, palms sweaty with excitement and fear, and many wet faces as the goodbyes were said to the family before going through gate A3 at the airport. I strapped in tight, felt the crying babies and chatter all about, with the occasional intoxicating smell of food items. Here we go, ready or not! Looking out the small oval window, knowing what was behind me: family, and what I learned. The blues and oranges faintly glowing through the airplane window in front of me. It was time to find my *group*, other Latter-Day Saints who shared the same values and beliefs.

Here I was, in a new state, with some extended family I did not know too well, but willing to take the chance, searching for friends, marriage, a sense of belonging, and future education, but overall brighter colors. As I walked into my new bedroom where I was staying, I allowed my body to fall on the bed in exhaustion from the emotional and physical strain of the latest and unknown. I heard a knock at my bedroom door, "Mindy, are you doing okay?" "Yes," was my reply.

My uncle entered the room and sat by me on my bed, and chatted for a few minutes about my next plan, my next move. Before leaving the room, he turned his head and stated to me in a very calm demeanor, "I have only planned the next day, but beyond that, it's up to you." No pressure, right? I was still an incredibly quiet and reserved young woman who just wanted to be associated with a *group*—where I could feel supported and loved and paint my canvas with brighter colors.

As I said before, my uncle did not have a plan for the following days and beyond. Still, I had a plan: first and foremost, to find my *group*. (I naively thought it would be easier because I would be around young people who mostly shared the same beliefs and values). I thought going to church activities and being around more people of my same faith would help. I was also going to nudge ever so slowly out of my safe bubble of comfort. After a few game nights and a few dates here and there, I managed to find a few good girlfriends.

I spent some Saturdays longboarding until the sunset rolled in. Every

Sunday, the smell of meatloaf or mashed potatoes would hit my nose, and for my ears, the classical rings of piano keys played from my friend's grandma's hands. I was always invited to my friend's family dinner, and it felt comforting being far away from home.

Then would come the opposite kind of days. I was standing in a crowded room filled with laughter, food, and my few friends roaming around the room, thoroughly engaging and having things to talk about. My heart racing, sweaty palms as I made my way around the room, getting up enough courage to say, "Hi."

Leaving the church building, I finally felt a sense of relief and thought to myself, "Maybe next time, if I just try to be extremely more outgoing or dress cuter, I'll make more friends. Or maybe a boy will notice me, and I would enjoy the activity better." College and working towards my Associate degree, always running from one place to the other with two jobs, consumed my life. Dark circles and fatigue crept up on me as I crashed on the bed, but it was worth it. I had a plan; I always had one.

Hear me out: the plan was excellent. While finishing my degree, I would look for a spouse who could do no wrong. I thought about starting a family while young. I thought life would be one of those movies where you see a happy couple running in a field of dandelions, swinging their kids high in the air as they giggled playfully. That was my vision at the time.

However, I continually went to activities whenever I could but didn't feel any difference in the friendship and relationship department. With the pressure of studying, working two jobs, and finding where I belonged, I would find myself eagerly grabbing the jar of peanut butter from the care package sent from home to sustain me during this period in my life.

I was reaching goals and "adulting." You see, what even made it more significant was one day, a friend's family member introduced me to this guy who was a Latter-Day Saint—like me. This person was the first young man to give me attention. Now that I think about it, whether good or bad, it was the affection that I had craved for so long.

The day came when I finished school and started working as a dental assistant. I loved being part of a helping team that made someone's day a little bit better. I also loved that someone of the opposite sex was paying attention to me; I now belonged to a *group* with a boyfriend. Times were good, except when they weren't with my boyfriend.

Life reminded me of the time we went to the amusement park—the light blues, yellows, and pinks on the gallant horses were going up and down and the smell of sugary sweet cotton candy. The day was filled with excitement as we waited in line to ride the zipper, holding hands. As we moved up in line, the tight, painful squeeze of my hand went up to my arm. The grip did not move. I looked over at him with a grimacing expression, and he had a smile for the world but eyes that only bore into me.

This was the first physical aggression directed towards me, while the shock that he could do it with so many people around was a red flag I ignored. Then I looked into his dark green eyes, searching for a reason as tears filled my eyes and his laughter at my pain killed my soul. I COULDN'T even find the right words to say. "What did I do wrong?" crossed my mind as the words from my boyfriend so easily slipped out like butter. "You weren't paying attention to me and loving on me enough. I needed to remind you where you should be focused at all times, and if you're not, I'll help remind you."

The painful reminder was the first that would be along my journey as I stayed with him. Remember, I now have a *group*, and I'm not going to go back to being alone. So with a deep breath, I smiled back through the digging pain to show him that I could rise to the challenge he had given me. While that was an easy fix, I thought it would never happen again if I just did one more thing next time in the affection department. Wrong, I was so wrong.

As the year went on, a few incidents happened, like holding on to me tightly until I would give in a little to sexual advances, or blocking the doorway. But, on the other hand, this person I had a trauma bond to, had a sizable family that shared my same values and beliefs. That felt right.

He was going to school and paid attention to me sometimes, which made it easier for me to downplay and rationalize his bad behavior for the perfect picture. I loved that I fit into society and the LDS church that pressured how life was supposed to go: attend school, get married young, and start a family as early as possible.

As we dated for a short time, I ignored the hole in his parent's living room wall and punching bag in the downstairs storage space as I walked past them every time for a family dinner, while it played out to be a "funny" story. I overlooked the accounts of coercion, like getting me in the back seat of a car to do sexual acts I was uncomfortable with and the threats of leaving me if I wasn't more affectionate.

The manipulation, control, Dr. Jekyll and Mr. Hyde, lack of empathy, and arrogant attitude were all red flags I saw sticking up in my canvas, like warning and danger signs. I nearly brushed them off every time I saw them. I figured it would be easier and safer to ignore and hope that he would get better. I could not predict what lay ahead for me. *The group,* I kept reminding myself. *You don't want to be alone* and feel the pressure of a young marriage and starting a family shortly after.

Our minds are so good at creating and holding on to a specific vision that sometimes we will endure pain and suffering at all costs because of a stroke of blue and yellow. Through the dark black paint, as I awoke each morning and throughout the night as so many moms do, my heart swelled with joy and laughter playing with my young child, but as the shadow of the night crept ever so closely in my world, fear, pain, and unknown crept in more and more each time.

The first few years of the marriage were challenging; what was supposed to be the honeymoon phase felt like a nightmare almost every day. I was scared to move or make any decision for myself as I didn't know what the punishment would be: physically, psychologically, or sexual. My spouse constantly judged my family from afar and stated, "They like me more than you," and questioned their values and beliefs. The brainwashing and manipulation to pull me away from my family worked like magic, ever so slowly. I went inside myself and only gave them little hints into my world, not enough for them to understand the big picture, because I was afraid of what might happen if my spouse found out.

The little bits I gave my family and in-laws were things like, my spouse said I couldn't go grocery shopping without him, but what was I going to do? I needed laundry detergent that day. Another time I let them in a little was when I was pregnant with my first child and preparing for my spouse's deployment for a year and being a new mom.

It was a typical day until the red rage splattered. A quick breeze of air rushing past my head and the cracking of split wood from the kitchen door pantry, as I thought to myself, "At least he missed my head." As I made the phone call, the words from the family went from comfort to "What did you do wrong?" or "Just let your spouse go fishing to cool down."

I was silently screaming for help, and no one around me was getting it! The only words I could get out between the salty tears were, "Maybe I *did* do something wrong?"

As a devout married LDS woman who loved God, the teachings, and the values of the LDS church (and still does), I brought my family to church most Sundays. As soon as my hand left the doorknob, the merging into another world occurred—Abuse.

I felt the weight of keeping my other world buried deep inside. Walking into the church building every Sunday, I forced the smile and persona of your typical happy family. We had our stuff together but had a few typical *marital problems.* Walking back into the house after going to church was like walking into another world. The question was, which one was true?

Until I could figure that answer out for myself, deep in my soul. Or until a therapist could inadvertently hear the silent screams for help. During this time I tried multiple therapists to "fix" the problem. The first therapist after the deployment didn't work because I was too terrified to open my mouth. I coped by writing in a journal almost every day. It was a place to put all the fear, pain, worry, and dark abuse that surrounded every other day.

Now, being a married Christian woman, I viewed divorce as the ugliest word you could ever hear! If I was not married, who was I? Was I just not trying hard enough? As society would have me think, the tightness of the body, the embedded lies that constantly circled in my head, the pain of light green fading into yellow bruises hidden from the world, were starting to make me question how much more I could endure staying in my *group.*

As I looked at my masterpiece, the sun was gone, while the clouds were constant. Something was wrong. I felt it in my bones; what was I going to do? I went to the only thing I knew then, to a second therapist, thinking maybe this time would be different. This therapist saw a hint of the gray as wetness soaked my face, but to me the pressure continued to build staring into the eyes of each other while holding hands during the sessions.

After a month or so, the therapist mentioned a support group when I got up the courage to go to a solo session. The splatter of light-yellow spread through my canvas and filled my soul with hope! I went one time to the support group but couldn't bring myself to go anymore. I couldn't take the psychological abuse when I returned home and heard "I was cheating while I was gone" or at an "Alcoholic Anonymous group." The splash of red was starting to cover the light yellow up.

I went back to this therapist a few more times solo until I got the phone call that stopped me in my tracks from the therapist, as she said. "Your spouse has stopped going, but I think you guys will be fine; he seems to be trying harder," I was a little shocked, and out of habit, replied, "Okay." I was trapped. Day in and day out, the pain was like weighted shackles that dragged heavy behind me and the silent voice no one could hear. Can you imagine screaming for 13 years? And no one hears you!

The rage and abuse died down a little, but that's part of the domestic violence cycle that is never-ending. Some immediate family was living in Utah, and I had a new little one on the way. I was hopeful that the picture of the well-put-together family would become something I could see as a reality and get a break from the imposter I felt like. Of course, there were happy times when we played with our oldest and just laughed while being a team. However, as soon as that moment died down, I felt a sick, nauseated punch to the gut every time, because I knew the abuse was just around the corner.

And there it was, the violent cursing and throwing of the leftover Chinese rice across the room; well, silly me, I cleaned up a little too early, trying to help. After about an hour of the rage in front of my oldest child, nauseated numbness would fill my body, but I would push on. I cleaned up and went to the park with my child to protect us and get away for a moment.

Every time the abuse happened, I never really fully knew why it happened or, worse yet, what I did to cause it or deserve it, as he would shout and hit with degrading blows. As a mom with a little one and one on the way, I stayed in survival mode to protect us. That became my mode of operation—survival.

I had my second child via emergency C-section from toxemia and from the stress of being verbally abused just days prior. The family had walked in on this particular incident as vulgar language spewed from my spouse's mouth because it was found out that I was attending a lesbian celebration of love. The blood drained from my body every time a family member walked out the door. I honestly did not know how many days of calm I would get, or how many days of locking my children in the room and me to play blocks to shield them from the truth would have to keep happening.

As time went on, I found a system that worked for my two young children and me. I played the game of walking on eggshells, didn't have a voice or desires, and only kept letting others in a tiny bit. Time had passed, and I welcomed my third child into this world, and that's when it became so dark and scary. The physical abuse got worse, with hard shoves in the back when not complying with sex, or the threats of leaving if I tried to work, make friends, or work out.

Eventually, friends, families, and strangers started to engage and ask the question bravely. Most are not ready to fully take on "What is going on?" in any way.

Slowly, the light blues, grays, purple and yellow I allowed others to put on the canvas of my life every day were mixing with the other colors. There was nothing I could do. Outsiders started to take deep notice, and it was too much work to cover up the emotional battle I fought constantly. I held onto the third therapist's card for about a week after Dr. Meacham kneeled in front of me and said the words I'll never forget, "Do you trust me, Mindy?" and handed me this life-changing card.

For the first time in a long time, I hoped that these two men could help me. I sat on my mother's bed with sweaty palms, tasting the salty tears as they hit my mouth, clenching the phone in one hand and a therapist's card in another. I knew with my heart beating out of my chest, I had to be fearless and act. This was my chance to break free of the chains.

I did. I called, but what followed was doubt, fear, and the constant threat of hearing, "If you walk out that door again with my kids, you better watch for red and blue flashing lights in your rear-view window." His never-ending threat.

The act of answering the call to action was so empowering, though; each session I went to with my third therapist, new rays of yellow and brightness overtook my canvas. This third therapist got it! He gave me the space, but he also pushed and forced me to acknowledge the truth every time I brought up a hint of abuse as the comforting words slipped out, "You are being hurt. This is not normal," and "I'm so sorry." He didn't blame me or force me to sit in the same room and hold hands while staring into the green monster eyes I knew.

I was still a bit in both worlds, though. The one where I went home every day knowing I was looking towards peace and happiness and holding on to it as tight as I could, but looking at my children and wondering to myself, "Could I face the stigma that came with breaking up a family?" I heard it more than I would like to admit from the LDS bishops when I would fearfully bring the abuse up. As I sat in the office with fear running through my body, the words, "Breaking up a family is the worst thing to do," struck my heart like a dagger. One day, as I was walking down the hallway to leave, a few ladies struck up a friendly conversation with me for a minute.

As the conversation went to our marriages and specific aspects of it were shared, the comment slipped out toward me, "Why don't you just try harder" I was taken aback by it and a little bit hurt in shock. The exciting thing about the thought of *Could I face the stigma of breaking up a family?* got easier week by week.

Within a short time, I started to loudly proclaim to my husband and the world, "I am going to work out," or "I am still going to take temp jobs in my field." I would also blast empowering music and hang out with other co-workers because it made me happy remembering the things I enjoyed so very much. With this, the pushback came hard and fast from the person who promised to love and respect me.

My actions had a consequence, and that was that I lived in fear that my children would be taken away, or my spouse would break through my bedroom door after spending nights locked in another room of the house to punish me. But I knew I needed to stand up against him.

Some local society and the LDS bishops proclaimed (not knowing the severity of the abuse) that if I just gave a little more grace or read the scriptures while praying more with my spouse, maybe I could fix everything. They just don't understand abuse. They think that you have a choice in having some control in your marriage. With abuse comes no control and no power, until that day comes when you know it is time to leave.

I remember feeling so frustrated with these people I shouted out loud, "If there is anyone out there who has a magic wand, please let me know; I would like to buy one!" Since I did not have a magic wand, my vision remained intact, which meant getting safe and taking time as a mom to go to therapy to address my anxiety and depression due to trauma. It meant going to work out at the gym or in a class, and every time I would work out, something extraordinary happened. I felt my mind was cleared because I was getting oxygen to my brain, and the happy endorphins were kicking in at full speed. When I did not go, the mental health that I needed to be there for my kids and myself would plummet.

As months and years passed, I was nearing the end of this exhausting battle of surviving. I started not to care if others liked my painting—my canvas. I felt I could finally break out of the cage when I looked at the colors, images, flags, deep darkness, and now splashes of power and energy. My cage was built by me out of debilitating fear, survival, and pain.

Mentally, I promised myself never to look back and made a pact with my third therapist that I was not going to look back. You see, in the past, I sabotaged myself by not fully committing to the dark and daunting task of actually leaving. One day, I made a second call to action, called the Domestic Violence Advocate, and opened up about what I was experiencing. A little bit at a time, I pulled some money out of our bank account and kept any money I made from my work in a safe—buying a few gift cards here and there. I firmly held on to my faith that God had a plan for my children and me, even though I couldn't see it.

Would I continue to let everyone around me paint the picture on the canvas that was more visually appealing to society, or would I listen to my intuition and paint a picture unique to me and my passions? I made a plan. I constructed it with therapists, family, and friends, and I executed it to get away from my husband. I was able to take my children with me. It was all due to the plan and the decision that I made that I needed to get away. God provided a way, and l left!

As a newly single mom, I was supposed to get a good-paying job where I worked long hours, did not see my three young kids, start school, and work to exhaustion while having no fun. It was sound advice, but there was something in my soul I could not ignore!

I felt the greatest desire to work at an elementary school, be on the same schedule as my kiddos, start writing my children's book that I thought about for years, and to get out there and test this new scary world I was entering in my way. "Why do you want to write a children's book? You're just finding random things to do," they said to me.

I chose to listen to my intuition and say yes to a publishing company that wanted my story and started writing it. Guess what! So many doors have opened for me with writing and speaking, and authentic, meaningful connections. What others do not understand they fear, and we have been trained to do things a certain way and use specific colors on our canvas of life to please others visually.

Writing has always felt like a blank canvas where I can create whatever I want, telling a unique story to my heart while potentially helping others. It was a vision unique to me that had many moving parts, but I was able to capture them through my words onto the canvas, and now I am free!

As time went on, I did not know what I was doing, but I knew if I did not have a vision of anything, I would fall off the track and be derailed. My new vision mainly consisted of being safe, happy, and healthy. Taking every opportunity that came my way if I thought it would be something I enjoyed and was part of my healing journey with purpose. Embracing the helpers and people God put in my life just at the right time.

I believe that everything happens for a reason, but the other half is listening to our intuition. It can lead us to that brightness on the canvas so we can feel the sunshine. Some of the "tools" that helped me live again and continue to live are to write almost every day in a journal and listen to empowering, uplifting music that has a message of hope for the soul. Exercising and challenging myself with 5Ks throughout the year also adds to my power.

I was scrolling on social media one day, and I crossed paths with the International Association Of Professions Career College on the internet. At the time, I did not know why I felt the need to do this two-month course and get a certificate, but my intuition told me, *this was something you should do!* Since that time, I have hung it above my desk as a reminder that motivation is an eternal part of all of us that we can work on every day.

With my new space, freedom, and life, my children started growing up. We had learning, joy without fear, and grace and forgiveness that helped us in our healing journey. One day, later in the afternoon in the summer, my kids were gone with their families. I did my typical routine: studying, writing, and taking a break to get my body moving. While I walked out of my bedroom and down the hallway, my intuition told me, go into my daughter's room. As I thought to myself, *Why? I don't have any reason to,* but I did anyway.

As I turned my head ever so slightly to the right of the room where my daughter had a full-body mirror, I saw the most beautiful words a mother could see. She had written with a bright green marker, "I am enough." My eyes scanned across the words over and over. *I am enough.* With a quick splatter of blue that calmed the heart and a splatter of green fly across my canvas, the cycle was being broken, and hope filled my soul for the future of how young girls and women should feel about themselves.

The flashbacks of eating my dark brown chocolate covering light brown peanut butter in my high school bathroom came to me. Instantly a rush of emotions came pouring through me. The wet, salty tears running down on my hot face and the very bones of my body feeling the wrench of my past, and delight in the example I was giving my young daughter. She would not run to a *group* just to "belong." She would not be trapped by the abuse. She was enough! She was enough!

Every young girl and woman should feel like they are enough. My pre-teen, who was about to enter middle school, watched me put mom first and learn this enormous statement. I think we all struggle at one time and feel that we are inadequate and not enough for this world just how we are. I did not have to say anything or preach anything; it just happened by observing my actions.

Periodically, my two oldest will write notes of affirmation or draw a pink, purple, blue, and green dragonfly because they know it's my favorite animal now. Last summer, I stumbled upon an article on one of those sleepless nights about the meaning behind the dragonfly that gave me a little AHA! moment. Therefore, in almost every part of the world, the dragonfly symbolizes change, transformation, adaptability, and self-realization.

The change often referred to has its source in mental and emotional maturity, and understanding the deeper meaning of life. Dragonflies spend most of their lives as nymphs below the water's surface and only exist as the beautiful dragonfly that we know for around six months, maximum. My desk area and room are now filled with self-care notes, and my visions for school, and the impact my children's book *Jane Leaps Through Headaches* will make in this world.

I still catch myself sometimes saying, "If I just try to do one more thing to fit in, will I be worthy of being part of that *group?*" When that happens, I imagine a dragonfly with *"I am enough"* glistening in its wings flying into my vision to help remind me that I belong because I am alive. I belong because I am loved. I belong because *I am enough!*

One thing I learned through my journey so far (because my canvas is not entirely done), the world needs the real you to shine through. From one woman who likes to bring one thing into a harmonious agreement with another, I know how hard trusting oneself can be and listening to that intuition, but it is a superpower!

If you have a vision, passion, desire, big or small, it was given to you to be manifested—so take action! Now I KNOW there will be days where the task will just be too overwhelming. Maybe the entire house is dirty, and it is too much to handle that day, or pure exhaustion sets in. I have days where this single mom gets overwhelmed, and my depression and anxiety take over. I must let it pass. Sometimes I cope while binge-watching a show and eating the whole bag of cookies or ice cream. On those days, I give myself grace, and so should you.

If you need to take a minute or a few hours to binge-watch that show, or curl up in the softest blanket while eating your favorite junk food, it's okay. If no one else permits you today, I do, my fellow warriors. But you mustn't stay long—just a short visit will do. Every day is a chance to take action towards your vision and passion, whether creating a new hobby or something on a grander scale. Breathe life into it and keep going so the flames do not burn out.

Life is our canvas, and just like if you were to go to a painting class, everyone's canvas would start the same: blank and white. But the more everyone painted, the picture would look different. How we decide to use the paintbrush, or our tools is our choice. We gain experience and color through our trials, pain, joy, hope, and passions. I know that we will ultimately create a masterpiece in the end!

All the smearing, splatter, and faint lines will manifest themselves, from looking basically as the messy part in the middle, to becoming valuable and beautiful! Those experiences shape the painting and who we are, and our purpose. Life would be pretty dull if we all had the same canvas. Not everyone will interpret or understand your masterpiece the same way, but they do say *beauty is in the eye of the beholder.*

My challenge to you today is to:

1. Have a vision, any vision at all, and write it down on a poster board.

2. Have external motivators that are unique to you!

3. Put them in every space where you spend the most time while looking at them daily.

4. And finally, believe in yourself—you are enough, and over time, you will see your masterpiece hanging up, and you will be surprised at the joy it brings to you!

Visit www.ncadv.org for National Statistics or to learn from the National Statistics Domestic Violence fact sheet.

Chapter 3:

The Process of Worship, a Journey of Judgement to Love.

By Michelle Saunders

Emotional Pancreas Protector

I would never accept a ride from a co-worker, but my husband was late to pick me up. However, on September 30, 2003, something told me to take the lift from my coworker Eugene. When he asked if I needed a ride, I told him I usually would wait for my husband, Greg, to pick me up from work, but I had been waiting for a long time. So, I accepted the ride from Eugene.

While on my way home, I thought about Greg. I thought about how he was super-focused while driving that he usually would drive past me. I would be on the sidewalk, and he would shoot past me and then park about thirty feet away. It happened nearly every time. He seemed always to be searching for something else while I was right there. That was an excellent description of our marriage.

You see, at this point in my life, I did not have my driver's license. I am a type 1 diabetic and was told growing up that I would not get my license unless I met specific requirements. Once I obtained it, I would need to go to the doctor to get a letter to the DMV to keep my license. I did not have time for that, so I relied on others for their support and transportation.

All of these things were knocking around in my head as Eugene drove me home. He would talk about the weather and other small-talk. It was nice. As we approached my home to drop me off, I thought it was weird that our truck was not in the driveway. "I wonder where he could be?" I thought. I opened the car door, turned and thanked Eugene, shut the door, and started walking up to my front door.

I pulled the key from my pocket, unlocked the door, and stepped into my home. I am usually bombarded by a four-legged bundle of energy, my dog named Sydney. However, as I walked in the door, I noticed Sydney didn't greet me.

I called out, "Sydney! Sydney?" No scraping nails on the linoleum floor, no bark, nothing followed my calls for the dog. Suddenly my eyes started to scan the living room. Chair, couch, table, computer—the computer was gone! This was strange, as Greg built the computer, but I thought he and Lisa had possibly taken it into Moscow, Idaho, to repair it. Trips like that happened occasionally, so I thought nothing of it.

Lisa. Lisa had a story. She was a friend who had to move back to Oregon the year prior, due to her mom's health. Lisa had a challenging life, and her plight fell on my heart. Lisa and I were friends, and I wanted to help. Greg and I discussed offering our spare room to her until she found a job and got an apartment with roommates to help her out. Greg agreed, and so, Lisa moved in the summer of 2003, when her mom no longer needed her help with her health.

I was thinking about all the great times Greg, Lisa, and I had on weekends—the pleasant atmosphere she seemed to bring into our home. My feet carried me out of the living room and down the hall toward our room. My eyes were still looking for Sydney, and my ears were listening for any signs of the dog.

I walked by Lisa's room. My eyes seemed to do a double-take. I noticed that all her clothing, minus the clothes that didn't fit me that I had given her, were gone—gone? Where were her clothes?

As I continued down the hall, my feet quickened. My mind started racing and making a list of the missing visual things: the dog, the computer, and her clothes. Suddenly I was facing the closets in my room. "What is going on? What was happening?" my head was saying, but my heart started to beat rapidly; it seemed to rattle against my chest. My trembling hand reached up to push open the closet door, and as I pulled it open, I found his closet was empty—all were gone.

Breathe, I commanded myself, breathe! My head spun as my feet circled me back to the front room, to the coat closet door that was slightly ajar. I had to see; I had to know. I opened the coat closet door—the dog food was gone. That was when it hit me that they had run away, literally.

I fell to the floor in tears. My mind was racing; my heart was breaking; I laid on the cold hard floor feeling broken—the vows, the promises, all if it meant nothing. In front of God and our families, he promised to be there for me in *sickness and in health, for richer and poorer*, and he left me. I felt like I was floating in the room and in the middle of a dream that turned from the happy-go-lucky carnival with balloons and rides to suddenly being on a rollercoaster, my buckle snapping in two, and me falling into a black hole of grief and pain. Images of my friend's face and his face flashed before my eyes.

I seemed to catch every glance, every sneaking smile that she and my husband had for each other. In this dark falling feeling, my mind was pulling up image after image of their flirtatiousness, which I mistook for friendship. I could hear their laughter, snippets of conversation, and smell her on the inside of my nose. I was numb. I couldn't feel anything. Floating was what I was doing. I was looking down at myself.

Being left behind in a marriage with not even the dog to comfort me was such a low blow. But it showed he cared about something. The dog would have faded away if he hadn't taken her. He left me scarred with memories because I acted as Jesus said to do, love everyone and treat them as you would yourself. Look at the payoff of that—a failed marriage, three years later - divorce and loneliness.

"This couldn't happen to me." I shouted out loud. "I had promised God to love and honor Him and my husband," I choked out over and over and over again. "I promised God! I promised! I kept my half, but Greg broke his vows. He left—and left with her!" My heart clung to that idea—someone I had tried to show love and compassion for had become the harlot—Jezebel. And Greg? He was just as guilty—if not more. That seemed to break a dam of new emotion. "God! God! Why did you allow this to happen to me?" I screamed out into the empty home. The echo seemed to bounce off each wall until it returned to me, empty. I called my small group leader from church, Nancy, and told her what I had discovered upon coming home from work.

She knew I was not in a place to be alone, and I spent the next week at her home. I had become part of her family. My church family took care of me for the next three weeks. I didn't stay at my home; Nancy and Stacey and their families took me in and provided me rides to work when I could go to work. See, I tried to go to work the very next day, but it didn't go so well. I told my line lead, and everyone was wondering why I would burst into tears. Eventually, I spoke to my supervisor and was told to take a couple of days to find out what was going on with Greg. Then I should come to work when I could function again. My church family and my work family were there for me as I worked through the grief of the death of my marriage.

Through that process, I learned that life continues to happen no matter the tragedy you've experienced, and you just have to pick up and keep going, even if all I could do was cry. The numbness of my body and emotions was as painful as open-heart surgery without anesthesia. How could I ever trust again? How could I extend love again?

I couldn't do it. So, I rebelled. I figured that God allowed this to happen, and I was going to turn my back on Him. I grieved the loss of my marriage by running away from the standards, morals, and all of my beliefs. I soon found myself on the other side of the equation. I had minimal moral standards, and soon, I didn't care. In my drinking and hooking-up-with-all-different-kinds-of-guys phase, there was someone who noticed me. There was someone who God sent to see me and get my attention.

"I know you are a believer," was all she said to me one day at work, with kind eyes and a smile. My heart skipped. I wanted to deny it. I wanted to yell back in her face that she was a liar! I tried to escape from it, but her words pinned me to the spot. I was caught. There was no more denying it, no matter what my recent actions propelled by all the pain felt; I could not deny it! I was a Christian. I knew better, but I was living the very painful lie of denying my heart and my testimony of God because I was so hurt. Pain and hurt can lead you to self-destruction—the very thing that Satan wants to have us all do—destroy ourselves.

My mind flashed with pictures and images from my past like a well-constructed PowerPoint. High school fashions, hair, and look—there I was talking, no wait, I was preaching. Look at me preaching the gospel to that girl in the hallway. Look at my passion and conviction as I tell them they are sinning. Look at me thump my Bible, and condemn peer after peer for what they were not doing—for all those sins.

With each memory, my gut started to twist and turn; I became dizzy and sweaty. As I saw my hand point towards my peers, I suddenly noticed how many fingers from my hand were directed back at me. Three—the Father, the Son, and the Holy Spirit. God wanted me to help others with a heart of love. Yet, I was pointing out and condemning those that were sinning. I was not showing them that if you love God, then keep His Commandments. I was running around like a judge saying, "Oops, you did that wrong. Oops, you broke the Fifth Commandment. Yikes, that's another bad mark against you."

I gasped when the last image that came sharply into my mind was of Shawn. I saw his beautiful face, his laughing eyes, and his good heart. Why can I see the good in him now and not back then? Suddenly, the next thing I see is my scorn of judgment and shame. It seemed to spew from my mouth all over him. I was horrible to Shawn, with my beliefs and lack of compassion in my heart for him and his salvation.

Shawn's lovely face was no longer smiling. His eyes were sunken, his cheeks sunk in, and his boney hand lay across his room temperature chest. The wet-faced mourners shared story after story of the beauty of this man, and I did not see him for the beauty of a spirit that he was.

I wanted to shut my eyes and turn away, but it was as if God was showing me my faults for a reason. I never even attended the funeral. This was all that I could see from my mind's eye. I would have never been found at his funeral because of Shawn's lifestyle decisions.

Why were my heart and mind creating this image in my head? I thought to myself. I instantly heard the words of my co-worker again, "I know you are a believer." The simple sentence that I heard in my mind repeatedly brought up all of this guilt and condemnation of my soul. I was caught.

I was a Christian who was judging others un-righteously. "Do not judge, or you too will be judged. For in the same way you judge others, you will be judged, and with the measure you use, it will be measured to you," Matthew 7:1 NIV. God showed my mistakes, judgments, fear, and self-righteousness—all as it were, in a flash of His time.

Finally, I saw the notecard. The simple $1.00 *My Condolences* written in deep blue ink across the jet-white card seemed to be covered with a layer of dust in my mind. I never sent that notecard. Why? Shawn was gay and had contracted HIV, which had progressed to AIDS. He wasn't the first gay man that I knew who was gay and passed from AIDS. My Uncle Perry, when I was twelve, passed away from AIDS because of his choices.

The final image of Shawn's name on the dusty card burned into my memory. Shawn was a son of God. I am a daughter of God. I had judged him, left him, and condemned him. I had condemned and judged all. I had never loved him. I then fell from grace and joined the conscious sinning. Who was I? I was no better than anyone else. I was not on a high and mighty pedestal looking down at others; I was here among them, with them because of my choices. Heck, we are all sinning—every day, we mess up. I had fallen based on all of my actions—especially following the divorce, and yet God still loved me.

God still loved me—how did I know that? How could God still love me? I had done nothing to deserve or earn His love. Then it hit me! God loves all of His children no matter the sin, and He desires that we will figure out our wrongs here and start finding Him to cleanse us and save us. No matter what, He still loves us!

Tears ran down my face as I felt His warmth surround me. I had sinned. I had messed up. Yet, I still felt His love. He was still here, I was still a child of God, and He would not forsake me. He still loved me. Those thoughts were clear, filled with light, and shoved the darkness from my heart that day. Again, the words of my co-worker were echoed back to me. "If you are a believer," for the third time, and I knew for sure that I was a child of God. Next, I heard and felt the Spirit whisper to my inner core, "As I have loved you, Love one another," John 13:34 KJV.

This event was a pivotal part of my transformation of learning to love all people, instead of judging those who didn't fit my mold of how people are supposed to be. Another scripture that resonated with me is found in Matthew 5:43-48 NLT.

You have heard the law that says, 'Love your neighbor' and hate your enemy. But I say, love your enemies! Pray for those who persecute you! In that way, you will be acting as the true children of your Father in heaven. For he gives his sunlight to both the evil and the good, and he sends rain on the just and the unjust alike.

If you love only those who love you, what reward is there for that? Even corrupt tax collectors do that much.

If you are kind only to your friends, how are you different from anyone else? Even pagans do that. "But you are to be perfect, even as your Father in heaven is perfect."

I had to learn to forgive and love Greg and Lisa, as well as his family, again. No, I would never be their friend or hang out with them, but I know that God loves them and has a place for them if they choose to follow and believe. God reminds me of how I lived growing up loving my great-grandpa as well as my grandpa. By the view of society, both men should have been locked away, beaten, raped, and killed for what they did to members of my family.

I was groomed by my great-grandpa. I visited my aunt and her family every summer for a week. We always drove into town to stay with my great-grandparents. Grandma and Grandpa would watch my cousin and me while my aunt ran errands. As a two-, three-, four-, and five-year-old kid, it was just part of how you interacted with Grandpa. You sat on his lap, and he'd tickle high up on your thighs; you would go out to the camper to get a piece of Juicy Fruit gum.

These things stopped when things happened, and it was discovered that we were not safe to be around Grandma and Grandpa without other adults. Grandpa went to counseling, as at that time in the early 80's he was given a choice for counseling or prison. I know there were more moving parts to this decision, but it was the decision made by my family. After that, our family set very strict boundaries to protect us from further grooming and abuse and stop the generations of sexual abuse in my family.

I still grew up loving both of my grandpas very much, but I knew they were not safe to be alone with them until I was old enough to protect myself. So learning to forgive and love Greg and Lisa was a lot like the process of learning new boundaries with my grandparents.

I had to cry out to God, and still do when I am hit with reminders of the pain from either instance, and sit on my Papa God's lap and just let Him envelop me with His love. I recognize people are hurt and affected by their childhoods, and that rewires how their brains work. They know what they are doing is wrong, but there seems to be telling them to hurt people anyways.

I also hold onto the fact that the ugliest, nastiest, vilest, creepiest criminal in the world is still loved by God. If God can love that person, then I can love the people who hurt me. It is hard some days, very hard, and those are the days that I talk to safe people about my life and the many traumas that happened to me. I haven't talked about all of them here. I also had the example of the generation before me in my family, who you would never know were traumatized as they were, because they got the mental help they needed to work through the pain, as I did.

They looked out for my generation and made sure we had the mental help we needed to deal with our traumas and showed us how to love those who hurt us the most. This doesn't mean we forget what happened to us, but we set boundaries for safety. Teach our children to protect their bodies and that we forgive others. Forgiveness is really for our hearts, so we can let go of the hurt and pain, so it doesn't eat us alive.

"Teacher, which is the most important commandment in the law of Moses?" Jesus replied, "You must love the LORD your God with all your heart, all your soul, and all your mind. This is the first and greatest commandment. A second is equally important: 'Love your neighbor as yourself.' The entire law and all the demands of the prophets are based on these two commandments." Mathew 22:36-40 NLT.

While at dinner, my friend put me on the spot and asked if I believed he was gay by choice or by birth. My response was, I believe it's a choice, conscious or sub-conscious, but it is not my place to judge you. It is my place to be your friend and love you. A childhood friend remembered how vocal I was about the LGBTQ+ community and what I thought those choices would lead to. For the next three years, I would go to Seattle to celebrate his birthday. Some of my favorite bars to go out to are the gay bars up on Capitol Hill to this day.

I believe that God created us to be heterosexual and that He makes no mistakes in His creation. That we are born what He wants us to be. Many people forget that He has given us free will to choose how to live our lives from the beginning of His creation. He has also given Satan the freedom to do what he wants on this earth.

We all have the power to tell Satan to "high-tail it out of our lives" if we choose. We can crush his head. But it takes strength to take on Satan. Even though we are created in His image, we have the agency to make choices and make mistakes that leave us corrupted.

The beauty of God is He *still* loves that corrupted person. He just wants us to choose to follow Him. This has been a long and arduous journey to figure out. I know I sounded elementary and *Pollyanna* right there, but I'm here to tell you that I am still learning. I am forever learning not to judge people and love them, mainly when they cause harm to me or a loved one. But I am living my life for Him, learning to do it with every breath I take.

Today, I am doing that and living my life the way I believe God wants me to be of service every day to others in His name. I now work with a beautiful group of women who come from all walks of life, all different belief systems, and together we are following the command to love your neighbor as yourself. Our group, Allies United for Change, peacefully protests various injustices in the world, and we do things to help the vulnerable in our community of Rochester, New Hampshire.

We have a 24/7 emergency pantry that anyone can access when in need. Renee, the founder of our group, met in the summer of 2020 to discuss some issues that the group was working on and then started talking about different ways to help the homeless. We talked about creating a pantry, and that was the first step in helping the homeless. We reached out to local churches to see if they would partner with us in providing a place to set up the pantry.

Grace Community Church heard about our pantry and quickly responded with a firm, YES! With their help, we started with a plastic outdoor yard cabinet that was top-heavy, and the wind blew over. It didn't survive. We were able to obtain, for free, a metal filing cabinet. So through the winter, we had a two-drawer and a four-drawer filing cabinet to stock for those in need. Grace Community Church had money donated to them to help us out, and an actual pantry cabinet was built. It is so big it is hard to keep it stocked full.

We have received negative feedback from a select few in our community complaining that they should help themselves; however, for the most part, we have found that most of our community supports us in our endeavor to help those in need. This cabinet is designed so that anyone in the community can go and purchase extra toiletries and non-perishable food items and leave them in the cupboard.

Creating the pantry is one sample of learning how to jump over my judgment of things and simply look at the needs around me and find a way to serve them. This has been my journey of learning to love and not judge; God has asked us to love and serve others. I find ways to do that. I didn't have to recommend the idea of a cabinet in our town for the homeless, but God wanted to help them, so I did. Others judge me because, heaven forbid, I help a drug addict. Guess what? God loves the drug addict, the homeless, and the fallen. I read story after story and parable after parable in the Bible of Jesus going and helping, serving, and loving them. Therefore, so must I. I can't turn my back on those who don't believe as I do; God loves them too, so must I.

I can't tell people, "You are going to hell for the way you live your life," as I used to in high school. Now I know that God doesn't do that. He gently guides His children to how He wants them to live their lives, which may differ from how I live my life. I am to be their friend and love them.

If I am asked what I believe in, I will always share what I believe—it is my testimony, and I won't deny it. I will never falter from that. However, I will always do it lovingly, as Jesus did with the woman at the well. (John 4) Even if they still disagree, I will still love them and still be their friend.

I have to thank God for the journey that He has taken me on to find how to love and help others, which I wanted to do in the first place. Now I know how to do it, and I will spend the rest of my life loving others and opening my heart to them, and no longer judging or condemning them.

Chapter 4:

The Path Not Taken

By Wendy Herrmann

Emotional Pituitary Contributor

"Do you have kids?" I was at a friend's housewarming party and standing next to one of their relatives, an older gentleman I'd never met before. We were engaged in some polite small talk, sipping a drink, awkwardly stuck next to each other while waiting for food and cake. I smiled and said, "No, kids aren't for us!" Inwardly, I rolled my eyes and felt a little sad.

I don't know this guy, and I was not interested in telling him my life story just to pass the time in the barbecue line. He remained stone-faced and replied, "Oh, I'm sure you'll change your mind." I nodded and turned away, fighting back the tears.

Growing up, I assumed I would want to have children and be a mom. Perhaps it was because that's what young women were *supposed* to want. Maybe I had not yet understood what was available to me as I grew older.

As the only girl of four children, I provided childcare to my two younger brothers on a part-time basis. I was a tween, and it usually occurred during the summer. I also did a lot of babysitting for others. As I headed to college, the thought of caring for young ones ever again started to sound more and more unappealing.

I found myself waffling on the desire to be a mother throughout my twenties. It often depended on who I was dating at the time; some men seemed more appealing as parental partners than others. Different relationships presented different paths. I was previously engaged, and he and I agreed that no kids were part of the deal. He is now married with children of his own.

Another past relationship would have led to moving to the East Coast, following my then-partner's academic career. He and I had talked extensively about having a family, and I believe it would have happened for us had we stayed together. Looking back, any of these paths would have lead to a fulfilling life.

My husband, Jon, and I married with the intent of remaining child-free. It was one of the foundational contingencies of our marriage. This is the type of thing you have to agree upon going in, right? We had initially not intended even to marry, as it seemed to fit best for parents. We could be together without being married and be in control of our reproductive choices.

"You know, people like you *should* have children," my medical provider said, while wrapping up my annual gynecological exam. She turned to me with a severe look. I had requested a refill on my oral contraceptives, as I never shared my decision to have children. She continued, "Both you and your partner are educated, stable, and healthy." Dumbfounded, I reiterated my determination, got dressed, and never saw her again.

I stewed on my way home. What did she mean? Was I somehow not fulfilling my duty as a woman? How dare she assume the decision to be a mother was one I took lightly. I made my decision *because* I am educated, stable, and healthy. I felt attacked and judged, as though her opinion of whether or not I *should* have children defined my worth. I carried that feeling of judgment for a long time.

A couple of years into our marriage, Jon came to me and said, "I think I want to be a father. What do you think about trying to have a baby?" Blindsided and speechless, my thoughts were spinning. I wanted to know where this was coming from. He continued, "I do not want to be older and regret not trying." Easy for him to say, he can procreate until he dies.

For weeks this hung over us, clouding our day-to-day interactions and everything else. It was all I could think about. I was anxious, terrified of what could happen. If I don't want to do this, is our marriage over? We all have the right to change our minds, and if this is what Jon wants, he deserves to have that with a partner who shares this goal. But I didn't want to lose my husband, and I didn't want a divorce.

While sitting outside by a backyard campfire, I tearfully asked Jon about what he wanted one night. I asked him about his previous relationships, questioning if the intent was to have children with any of them. Had he pictured this in his life all along? Was he lying to himself and me when we agreed on this before marriage?

He asked me the same thing, and I recalled those previous relationships and how each one presented different options and paths. I couldn't tell if this was helpful or muddied the waters even more. How can we know whether or not our minds will change again? It's not like you can send the kid back; this is a lifetime commitment. I hated feeling like it was all on me to decide for both of us. The pressure was overwhelming, and I feared Jon would resent me if I opted out. Even worse, I feared resenting myself, preemptively feeling regret for either choice.

After a time, Jon came to me and said, "I choose our marriage above all. If you do not want to try, I accept that, and we will have the child-free life we had planned on." I know he gave this real thought, and his words were genuine. This also gave me complete freedom, to be honest about what I wanted and feel safe in whatever I decided. The pros and cons of this decision were equally weighted. I imagined a child-free life full of travel, adventures, and an advancing career. At the same time, parenting would bring all those things, just in a different way. There were no guarantees either way that it would be awesome or horrible or neither or both. After all the inner debate, I decided: I wanted to try.

At this point, I was thirty-five years old, and the thought of starting this process, especially a technique I thought was never going to happen, was overwhelming. Over thirty-five, and the label is "geriatric" for pregnancy. Ouch. I had not lived a life preparing my body for childbearing.

As a life-long learner and researcher, it was time to dive into this adventure. I met with a new OB/GYN and learned what I needed to do. I spent the next few months getting off birth control, letting my body return to a natural cycle, and understanding how to track ovulation and fertile windows. It was time. We were heading out for a trip to Costa Rica and agreed we would start trying when we got home.

Lying in a hotel bed the night before the early flight to Costa Rica, my thoughts were racing. I turned to Jon and said, "I don't think I want to try for a baby. I can't do it, and I don't think I want it." I can't remember what he said back to me—something reassuring with the overall message of "yes we can" or "you can do this" as he held me close. I nodded and tried to sleep.

That trip was amazing and only slightly tainted with my perpetual second-guessing. We were there with others from across the U.S. in my husband's line of work. He would talk shop with colleagues, and I would find spouses to chat with. One evening, I stood next to a corner table in the Costa Rican hotel bar, trapping those sitting there and sporting a white wine-fueled expression of self-doubt, as if I was the first woman ever to question this decision. I found myself weighing my pros and cons out loud, searching their faces for some sort of answer. Indeed, across this table of older and wiser women was someone who knew the truth, the right words to give me the validation I desperately needed.

There were a few standard replies along the lines of "Parenting is so great!" and "Everyone wants to be a mom, it's so rewarding!" and "You won't regret it!" Perhaps seeing the need to save me from myself in the context of this conversation domination, a very kind woman leaned over, patted my hand, "You'll do great, dear." It was exactly what I needed to hear. And I believed her.

I got pregnant the first month we tried. The overachiever in me felt pretty smug, and there was some self high-fiving. The weekend before my first doctor's appointment, I started bleeding and then cramping—oh, the cramping! The blood loss and *next-level pain* were all I needed to know this pregnancy was over. My husband called our neighbor, his sister, to sit with me while he went to Walgreens for pads and supplies. She sat next to me on the bed, and I looked at her through tear-filled eyes. "I didn't even get to tell you I was pregnant yet. And now I'm not."

We kept that first medical appointment and went together. I wanted to talk to the doctor to understand how to care for my body and what we needed to do before we considered trying again. The nurse entered the small waiting room with an enthusiastic "So... you're pregnant!!"

"Nope," I replied, "I miscarried over the weekend and want to talk about what to do next." The constant professional switched over to problem-solving mode and said, "Let's take some blood and check your hormone levels; that will tell us where you are in *recovery,* and we can talk about the next steps." I looked over to Jon as the word *recovery* echoed in my head. Recovery implies there was something to get over, to give time to heal. This was not something I took into account when we started this process.

"You were early in your pregnancy," she continued, "a very common time for miscarriage, and something very manageable." When she returned to the room with my lab results, she noted that my hormone levels told a different story, indicating I was still pregnant. "Sometimes, it takes time for these levels to come down. Let's do lab work again tomorrow and see where you are at."

Tomorrow? Was I going to have to return tomorrow? I looked at Jon, and he gave me a *let's-return* sort of look. The subsequent blood work the following day indicated higher hormone levels. *Higher?* I didn't get it. My uterus was empty; how were the levels higher? My husband and I looked at each other, trying to decide if we were scared or just confused. "We need to do an ultrasound and take a look."

The ultrasound I had in mind involved jelly on the belly, that weird handheld scanner thing, and looking at a screen. And it started that way. However, to get a closer look, the transvaginal ultrasound wand was brought out. If you've never experienced what I now refer to as the "trans-vag," I do not recommend it. It is invasive and uncomfortable; however, in this case, it was *extremely* necessary.

The ultrasound indicated swelling in one fallopian tube, implying an ectopic pregnancy. An ectopic pregnancy occurs when the traveling fertilized egg does not make it to the uterus and grows in the wrong spot. According to my body, this was still a pregnancy, hence the increased hormone levels. Slight swelling in my other fallopian tube showed a chance of a dual ectopic pregnancy.

Later, my doctor explained: "Because of the uterine bleeding, along with swelling in both fallopian tubes, it may have been a triple pregnancy. We will never know for sure." *Triplets*—was all my mind could shout. Triplets? At that moment, we felt like we dodged a bullet. Again, *Triplets?* I don't think so. My mind continued to picture my ovaries just throwing out as many eggs as possible (a common physical occurrence for older women), seeing who would get lucky—kind of like one of those t-shirt cannons at basketball games.

Awaiting results and next steps, Jon and I needed lunch. While Jon drove, I called my work to ask for help with getting a message to my students regarding my absence at a pre-planned event that night. Doing my best to keep my voice calm and clear, I said I had a family emergency and was needed elsewhere.

The practical side of me was checking off all the things that needed to be taken care of, while the stronger, emotional side knew nothing else mattered, and why am I not sharing the truth? My mind was a tornado of thoughts and feelings; it felt chaotic, and nothing could hold it down.

Jon and I ate in silence. We didn't have anything else to say as we were just waiting for the next piece of information. Then I got a call. We were needed at the clinic as soon as possible. Can we get there within the hour?

Because my hormone levels continued to rise, treatment was needed immediately—*treatment.* Untreated ectopic pregnancy can result in rupture, internal bleeding, loss of fertility, and even death to the mother. The treatment for my ectopic situation was to receive injections of the drug methotrexate. This drug is often used to treat cancer, rheumatoid arthritis, or multiple sclerosis. The thought of this going into my body freaked me out.

After two injections in the gluteus, the doctor sat with me and went through instructions for when I got home. "We are trying to destroy cells that are growing, so it's important that you remain still and avoid green foods or anything *healthy* that typically encourages cell growth," she said. Did I just get permission to lie on the couch and eat potato chips—on doctor's orders? Finally, some good news.

She continued, "Also, you mustn't get pregnant while this drug is in your system. Do not try. I'm asking you to take birth control pills to cover all our bases." After following all the protocols to get off birth control before commencing this journey, I was disappointed and felt like everything was going in reverse.

"Go to the lab for blood tests every other day. We need to check your hormone levels to ensure they are going down, and the drug is working." Jon looked at me and took my hand as we walked out. I remember him saying, "It will be okay." I don't think he knew what else to say. Neither did I.

A few days later, I got a call. "While your levels are evening out, they are not dropping at the rate we are looking for. You need to come in for a second dose."

All of this seemed so clinical, and at the same time, I needed to face the loss of the pregnancy. I got so wrapped up in my physical recovery; I kept pushing that grief aside. As the methotrexate started working and my hormone levels were coming down, I asked Jon how he was doing with all of this. It was his loss, too. "We can always try again. I was more worried about losing my wife." Oh, my heart.

The recovery took months for my hormone levels to return to normal, for us to accept what had happened, to tackle the grief and the fear of going through this again. Hovering over this experience was the powerfully negative emotion of shame; in crept the doubt and the barrage of fear. I thought, *a woman's body is built to do this, and I failed.*

I didn't tell many people. I asked those who knew my situation not to tell others, and I could barely say the word *miscarriage* out loud. The idea of parenting fell to the wayside. My defenses were up; maybe not wanting children was the right thing. Look what happens when I try! Why did I set myself up for this?

A couple of years later, I sat Jon down and said, "I think I want to try again." This time it came from me, and Jon was surprised and excited. He didn't want to pressure me and admitted to feeling guilty about pushing the idea in the first place. Neither one of us could have predicted what would happen, and as much as we sought answers, there was no place for blame when it comes to things like this. We agreed to give it another shot.

Again, pregnancy came easy within a couple of months of trying. Being even older this time around and with an ectopic history, I was classified as high risk from the start. I was seeing a new doctor and was upfront about my history. As soon as that test was positive, the doctor had me come in to confirm the pregnancy was in my uterus, and we weren't facing another ectopic situation. I got to hear the heartbeat that day and was flooded with relief and joy. I scheduled a ten-week check-in and was ready to move forward.

The ten-week ultrasound revealed no heartbeat, no pregnancy, and intense devastation. My heart went out to those I know who have faced this many times. How do they do it? I felt so useless and like such a failure. I remember sitting in the waiting room with Jon, my head on his shoulder, as we processed the news of the loss.

The doctor suggested I wait for my body to pass the miscarriage naturally and give it a few days. A week later, unable to stand the waiting, I scheduled a dilation and curettage (D&C) to bring an end to the process.

A few days later, I sat in a human resources orientation at my new job, straddling an industrial-sized pad, waiting for the expected heavy bleeding to begin. I constantly held back tears, knowing my body was trying to process immense hormonal changes and also knowing how sad I was.

What was wrong with me? Why couldn't my body get this right? I was surrounded by people who had no idea what I was going through, and I silently sat in my pain and grief. We got to the benefits piece about maternity leave, and I had to excuse myself. I hid in the bathroom and wiped my tears, enduring the onset of cramping.

After a moment, I pulled myself together and rejoined the group as if all was fine. I hid the entire experience from my coworkers; doing so allowed me to compartmentalize my pain. At work, I could pretend I was fine, masking my shame and embarrassment. My perpetual people-pleasing tendencies didn't want to make a new acquaintance uncomfortable. It was easier for everyone to pretend this wasn't happening.

After a few months, I sat Jon down one more time. "I don't want to do this again. I cannot handle this level of pain and blame and sadness." He agreed, and we celebrated that we tried. While this brought an end to the physical aspects of pregnancy and loss, the long-term processing of grief, trauma, and self-blame was just beginning.

As someone who struggled with feeling like I was *enough* in life, I viewed the inability to carry a child as the ultimate failure. If I could not do the thing my body was designed to do, would I ever be *enough* at anything else? I went back to school, lying to myself that a higher degree would prove that I was worthy of having space in this world. I questioned myself often, unable to trust that my decisions and actions would work out.

Instead of seeking support from others who have lost pregnancies, I reminded myself that I didn't want kids in the first place, so this shouldn't hurt so much. I should be able to "get over it" rather quickly. I kept my feelings of shame, failure, and grief from Jon because I should know how to feel better.

I was shoulding all over myself. And I was hurting. In hindsight, I wish I had sought out support from others who shared this experience.

As time has passed and I've opened up to others, I have found great comfort, solace, and relief from the burdens of grief through this open processing with others. I remember seeing a friend who shared she had just suffered a miscarriage for an unexpected pregnancy. I reached out and took her hand, asking her why she didn't call me. She didn't want to remind me of my loss by sharing hers. This is a telling way of how women take care of others, especially regarding loss and grief.

Years after my multiple losses, my close cousin called me to tell me she was pregnant. This was not in her plan, and she was scared. She texted the first ultrasound picture, and I smiled with so much joy for her. And then I cried, collapsing onto Jon with exhaustion over such an unexpected emotional response. A couple of months later, I saw her, and she shared how scared she was to tell me.

Here she was experiencing something I couldn't, and she felt guilty. I rubbed her belly and said, "My sadness is not more important than your joy, just as your joy is not more important than my sadness. We can experience both together."

Later she came to live with me when her son was born, invited me into the room, and let me witness the birth. This experience changed me, giving me a glimpse into the background and providing a sense of closure I didn't even know I needed. I am forever grateful to her for that.

Grief is complicated, and it lingers. I am fortunate to have mental health support, a caring therapist, and the desire to get better. I strongly believe in the efficacy and necessity of therapy to help us process the ups and downs of life. I started treatment with a short-term plan to help with some decision-making that has blossomed into years of deep work, revealing the layers of my life experiences and understanding myself.

I was/am privileged to have access to this type of care, and the luck that comes with finding a great match with my therapist. This work helped me build a foundation that did not lessen the pain of this experience but did help me move through it with healthy tools.

Through this work, I learned about the post-traumatic stress that comes with pregnancy loss and how that can be even more intense when the physical aspect gets serious, like ectopic pregnancy. With continued self-reflection and therapy, I found my worth exists simply by being here on this planet.

During one intense session, I recall saying, "I just want this to be over; I don't want to feel sad and worthless anymore. When does it end?" Her reply, "Instead of asking when will this end, let's look at it another way. When will you start forgiving yourself? When will you start giving yourself support and kindness? What would you say or do for a friend in this situation?"

She reminded me that there are many parts of life where we have to choose one way. We cannot have all things in all forms. Sometimes we have to grieve the path not taken as we embrace the one we are on.

I remind myself of this exchange quite often. Instead of thinking this is something to "get over," I let the feelings come, give myself space to process, and remember that this is part of who I am. I forgive myself for the blame I carried. Being gentle and kind to myself helps me be that for others.

My sadness comes and goes and continues to lessen over time. I will always carry it with me. We learn to live with grief, and I can now use my experiences to talk to others and share the complicated meaning of being a woman. This experience is part of who I am and an intricate part of my return to the desire not to have children.

Sometimes, I see moms with kids and think about what could have been. It does look like fun—helping someone learn and grow, watching them figure things out, providing guidance, and understanding that level of love and trust. What if we kept trying? Would it have worked out, and I'd have a little one now? Would it have been lost again and again?

I'm not sure my heart could handle either of these options. At the same time, I see my life without children, the freedom it affords, the depth of my marriage, the opportunities to work on myself, and I am filled with joy. I'm learning that my authentic self is always enough, with so much to offer. I find fulfillment in helping, teaching, guiding, and encouraging others to find their best.

I get asked about motherhood often. I used to be upset by it, reminded of the loss over and over. In time, this has lessened, and I can take it for what it is. It's one of those questions that come up when we meet people. Usually, I respond with "Nope, child-free for me!" or "I have a cute dog, Penny, do you have kids or pets?" or "It wasn't in the cards for us." These replies are easier than diving into the story, the not wanting, the trying, and the loss and ongoing grief. It's a lot to expect someone else to process.

The next time you meet someone new, consider this: be gentle in asking about personal things. Instead of asking about kids, ask about hobbies, how they spend their time, what brings them joy. Understand that we all have different triumphs and struggles and consider your words when these topics come up. If someone shares, they have experienced pregnancy loss, a simple "I'm sorry" goes a long way. Give space for them to share their story, or not. Respect what is said, the tears that may come, or the subject changes to talk about something else. We are all carrying things in our way.

As women, we face many external pressures and expectations to follow a path, fit in with others, or do things a certain way. The truth is, there is no "way" to do life.

There are so many ways to experience parenthood. I am thankful to those who sit with me in grief, who acknowledge that my experience is shared by many. I celebrate those in my life who foster children, those who welcome exchange students, and those who spoil their nieces and nephews. I applaud those who show up at the neighbor kid's ball game, who give parents a much-needed night off, who overspend on the latest ball team fundraisers, who are kind to the tired baby in the check-out line, and all who remind each other that we are doing the best we can.

"Do you have kids?" My honest answer is not a simple one. I do not have children. But I am a mother to all the children in my life, to my friends and family, to my sweet dog, and to the spirits of the ones I lost. I carry this with me as part of who I am, proof of my resilience and ability to grow, and as a reminder that we all walk our paths our way.

Chapter 5
Finding the Positive Roots to This Ghostly Tree
By Lisa Nelson
Anxious Balanced Builder

Finding the Tree

I sat at my desk with a quizzical look on my face in a state of wonderment. My first-grade teacher was telling us to create a family tree. I thought to myself, *A family tree—to find out the meaning of my last name? Well, this is dumb, because my last name is not my real name.* This assignment did not make sense to me. That is not my actual name.

Why was the teacher asking me to be someone that I was not? Why was I using a name that was not even mine? You see, I was adopted. My brother was adopted, and our adoptions were both contrasting situations, four years apart. We were just two children who happened to look similar to our parents.

Growing up, my parents seemed to be each other's soulmates. Both of them were always the first to step up and offer their services to others. They were a fun-loving couple that was very much in love and wanted to give two children a better life. I felt very loved by them but was just always confused as to why my birth mother and father gave me up for adoption in the first place. It left a hole in my soul, and I desired to know who I was. It is an abandonment and separation thing. Like when someone who used to be friendly or romantic with you suddenly cuts off all communication without explanation. That can leave you feeling confused, hurt, paranoid, and again abandoned.

Most adopting families will give you whatever they can to make a new family for the one they could not naturally have. It seemed as if they were hyper-aware of making sure that you felt special and accepted. Even though your parents are very aware that they have raised you with acceptance, this internal feeling of never belonging persists.

My Ghost Kingdom

It's a feeling like I am walking around with ghosts. These ghosts hang around my family tree, trying to connect to me. There is a feeling of ghosting related to closed adoptions, which was a much longer and deeper process for me to work through.

The ghosts in my kingdom are impressions. They are an echo or a feeling of somebody that once was, but they are not terrifying. They're still helpful when they come to visit. You don't even know them, but you start to learn more about them through these eerie ideas. So how do you know if they are telling you the truth? What or who should I believe? My family tree was rootless because there was no one else in it—but I had to come from somewhere!

My identity was attached to a sense of belonging, usually through family ties or deep emotional connections—that is true for nearly everyone. Since I did not have that, my ghosts appeared. I would get aggravated quickly and stay in my own space, isolated and hiding in my bedroom, living in my secret little ghost kingdom.

However, there is another type of *ghosting*. This ghosting comes from being rejected and not knowing why, even when you thought you were in a relationship; or you "thought" you had a friend or family. I would exclude myself from others. Rejection abandonment would happen again.

So I created a family tree and a ghost kingdom that would give me comfort. It was filled with abstract animals and friends on my exclusive tropical island of creative mirages. It was my hypothetical world of freedom and power that I would enter when imagining my birth relatives. They would wander around my family tree, and there were times when I would try to connect with them and ask them how they were connected to me. I was never afraid of my kingdom. Those imaginary ghosts are always encouraging, and they try to get you to keep going. My kingdom was full, and no one else could see them.

I would leave my kingdom to engage in the real world. But two questions were constantly revolving in my mind. As I watch people at the store, at school, or even at the mall, I think: *Am I related to you?* or *Who are you to me?* This constant sense of disconnection or not knowing where I came from seemed to control my life. What if I walked past my biological parents every day and never knew it?

As I watched people, I thought *I must be related to the gal over there on the other side of the room because we have a similar hair color!* Or I would be doing an art project and think, *I have a very creative mind; I wonder if that comes from my mom or dad?* I would also think, *Maybe my birth mother was Georgia O'Keeffe?* I also loved music, and I wondered, *Was my birth father a famous singer?*

These thoughts helped me to develop the ghosts that would wander around me. They were my family. For anyone who is adopted, just think, you can make your ghost kingdom be *anything* that you want because of the veracity of it all.

Forests, Ghosts, and Health Challenges

I also wanted to know who my family was because I have medical challenges. I wanted to know my genetic makeup to understand why I dealt with these issues. Medical concerns started at a very young age for me, and then as I got older, hormones kicked in and threw things off abnormally even more. If I had to go into the hospital for something, they probably did not know what it was. They would just tell me that it was likely just growing pains. In college and becoming an adult, it was even inadequate. And other extensive concerns were handed to me, so there were always unanswered questions in my mind.

Many other things could be worse than being adopted. Life was given to me, and that was a blessing. Everyone has their own story or reality. They might disagree with it, but they deal with it. For me, I wanted to find and fill the gaps in my story. So I created or collected faces and ghosts to be a part of that kingdom. I just want to know them and learn more about my birth family.

I wanted to find a way to fill that gap of the unknown and find a way to connect things to help figure myself out. Children brought up living with their birth parents most likely have imaginary friends—I mean, I think that is normal. But in due time, these friends fade away as they grow up. They stayed around longer for me because I wanted to fill in the gap with this fictional world. After all, I was not allowed to discover the world of my birth parents.

I wandered in crowded areas, again ever-thinking that maybe my birth relatives were there. Each stranger could be a potential family member. I even worried that I might unintentionally sleep with a half-sibling. What if I saw vaguely familiar faces? I would always wonder and then think, *What if?* Because there was no way to trace my origin, I learned from my personal medical history and created my roots.

Everyone is unique and paramount in their particular way. Many people brought up in a closed adoption have questions about themselves, medically, genetically, physically, and mentally. Anyone who is adopted is going to want to know who they are if they are inquiring. Many will want to explore that idea—I did. I wanted information and answers to my questions. Without having these explanations, I felt hollow and empty. I longed to know who I was and where I belonged. Not knowing who you are can be wounding. Wounds like this took place in my early brain development, and it got rewired.

Because I craved belonging so much, it gave me two unique skills. I can easily create friendships and groups wherever I go, and I can sense others who have walked in the same shoes. When you meet others who have walked in the same shoes, you will know it. Instinctively, I seem to know when someone has been on the same wavelength. My intuition kicks in, and I can tell when someone knows what I am explaining to them because they have been in similar situations.

I never hid the fact that I was adopted, and neither did my parents. In sixth grade, we had an assignment to do a small talk in front of the class for the first time, and I chose to speak about it. And I am sure that made a few others in my class realize that I was adopted, but it was not that obvious. My parents always wanted us to know that we were adopted because they wanted to be honest and open about it and even encouraged it. It was never a punishment. It was always a blessing.

For me, growing up in a small community offered blessings for a girl creating belonging. I loved to try anything that was a team effort, so I chose to be in every group, sport, music, or art venue that I could. And if I did not like it, then I would undertake a different one! So there was almost always a friend or athlete who wanted to connect or be a team player! Even later in life, I loved to volunteer and help others; and in college, I took on many other clubs. I think that was my inner drive to meet part of my family. So, I was always getting involved as much as possible in the hopes that I would connect with them.

If I found anything that sparked my interest, I would explore it more, and I tended to make friends wherever I would go. My companions' experience seemed to grow, and I noticed they would ask me things they could not ask others. Anyone who has experienced *outsider* feelings; they were drawn to me.

Over time, I tried to create friends and family wherever I went. Whether it was taking art classes, going to concerts, dancing, or having dinner with others, I was just having fun with new people. Then I started having many different friend groups, some older and some younger. I am pretty accessible to others, and I want to be friends with whoever wants to be friends with me.

That is not to say that I just always accept everyone. Boundaries are critical. For example, if I am lied to, or when a partner puts their own needs and desires ahead of what is best for us or our relationship, my trust in them is damaged. Violating important expectations, or if it seems like the top of that jar just is not fitting right, then I do not feel like they are worth my time. I am not going to try SO hard to pop that balloon just to let it blow up in my face! I can feel it when others are lying, and I am not going to bullshit anyone. I just move on.

Finding More Trees in my Forest

Making friends in a small community became simple, but what would I do alone, a thousand miles away from where I grew up? That was a big step, because I had always lived in Wisconsin. It felt like a new beginning, of sorts, and my brother's roommate had just left, so there was an open room. I lived in California for a while to break free from a time in my life where many things had collided. Work complications, health issues, relationship troubles, and our mother's passing had all happened within one year. It was all very overwhelming!

When I lived in LA, I truly enjoyed working at a well-known sushi restaurant in Hollywood. As the sun would set, the building was a vibrant red, with the front corner of the building looking like a billboard facing Hollywood Boulevard. There was a large visual of a woman's mouth with chopsticks in it, and the lips had bright red lipstick on them. There were also lit squares on giant screens that would draw people in by randomly flashing colors of lights.

A sign positioned above the mouth was small, electric text, two words: Geisha House. It was always an exciting night because you never knew who would show up; actors, actresses, and musicians, some very unexpectedly. During dinner, one or two ladies wore kimonos, and they had beautiful personalities and would greet others. Their regalia was beautiful, T-shaped, wrapped-front garments with square sleeves—white facial makeup with red lipstick, broad sashes, zori sandals, and Kanzashi traditional hair ornaments.

Even if the doors were open, the entrance was pretty hidden, and if you had not been there before, you would most likely walk right by it. There were a lot of secret exits from all sides of the restaurant. The main entrance was just a tiny side door with a few flat black curtains draping down. Next to that, I stood in a small space, essentially answering the phone behind a vibrant Japanese-designed counter space. My view consisted of a hallway entrance resembling the mesmerizing red *torii* gates, like those in Fushimi Inari Taisha in Kyoto, Japan.

I had not worked there long, and randomly one evening, someone's head popped through the little black curtains on the door. The individual says to me, "Is this a *real* Geisha House?" I started laughing and explained that it was a sushi restaurant. He said, "Oh, wow! That is so much better. I was a little worried there for a second!" We laughed and just started chatting. We talked for about ten minutes. He was from the East Coast, visiting some friends, and was just in town for about a week.

I had to get back to work, but he said, "I had a friend of mine drop me off, and I do not have a vehicle while I am in town."

Without hesitating, I said, "I am pretty new to the area and rarely have time off, but I need to learn more about the city! Would you want to go for a drive tomorrow afternoon and do some exploring?" We had a beautiful day riding down the coast and exploring things that I had never seen before! I have stayed in contact with him ever since. I have learned that anywhere I seemed to go, I could make a new friend pretty quickly.

Uniting the Trees in my Forest

It was not the only cross-country move I ever made. Some people have said that it was brave for me to move without knowing people. Who is brave enough to face the unknown? I think that you are brave enough when you live life to the fullest with conviction, free from the weight of affliction. It challenges you to get real, but at the same time, you never know what to expect.

I got it from being suddenly cut off from all communication without explanation, and because of epilepsy that has haunted me for most of my life. I never know when I will have a significant seizure. And I always get a kick out of it when someone says to me, "Just think positive, and that feeling will just disappear. You will forget all about it!" Wow! Are they ever wrong! You can try with all of your might, but no matter what you do, a seizure will step in out of nowhere and sit in the pit of your stomach!

I feel like, over time, I have learned to step it up a bit and try not to judge people because of invisible illnesses. Everyone has a personal situation to deal with, and there will always be something that will try to hold you back. Not everyone will hear you when you open up to them, and I will just tell others what I know from experience. No one will ever know everything that another individual has been through. In the past two years of my life, I have learned that, even if I do not need help, I feel better when I am at least offered assistance or acknowledgment.

I have another friend of mine who did not tell anybody about his seizures. I have known him for about fifteen years, but he did not feel comfortable opening up to his family for quite a while. I had already been dealing with epilepsy for the majority of my life. I told him that by not telling anyone, it might eventually become a life-threatening issue. I mentioned, "You could have something happen in a family or public setting and not know it because you can go unconscious."

He had no response, so I pushed on. I explained to him that I was thinking about having brain surgery to help control my epilepsy. He audibly gasped. Now, it was not like I was flippant about that decision. It was a vast choice that I had to make, but it was the next considerable step in my life. "Brain surgery?" he responded. "I cannot understand why you would do that."

"Well," I replied. "I have been suffering for a few decades with seizures. I am kind of done with the whole thing. And, to be honest, I do not have many options left." He started to understand.

A few days later, he rings again to ask more questions. "I have another question for you. What does the XR mean on the prescriptions, because I am confused?" he said.

I responded, "Funny you should mention that, because I have been in that situation myself." I said, "I believe you are having the problems because you DO NOT have extended-release tablets, aka XR." He was surprised, so I pushed on. "You need to call and tell your doctor that you need those back, to help your body stay at a steady level for longer periods," I said.

"What do you mean?" he asked.

"The XR stays in your system and does not just flush out of your bloodstream right away. You are most likely having seizures right before your next prescription is due to be taken." He was stunned that I even knew that. I was glad that I could help him.

You see, I want anything I have learned with my medical challenges to help others. And I am always happy to assist. I have kept daily journals of almost every health issue I have had for the last ten years. I want to grasp from what I have recorded in my journals and see progress!

My friend is now starting to have more seizure issues, similar to what I had described in my past. He eventually learned quickly after multiple occurrences that what I was saying was helpful. I was glad I could support and advocate for him. I have found over the years that many people do not want to own their medical challenges, and play the victim.

There is a lot of shame around having seizures. People can become embarrassed that they cannot control it, cannot fight it, and they just happen when they happen. Many never want to tell people about it. Because underneath all of it, I feel, they do not want to take responsibility for it. They do not want to look like a wimp, or if they are professionals, they do not want to lose their license, because they work hard and have to drive to clients. I get it. However, they will eventually realize that they do not have control over these. The feeling of having no control over something... that is just asking for unrest!

As I meet other people and try to describe everyday situations with epilepsy, some are ready to hear, and others, it is not the right time to learn. They can *hear* me speaking, but they do not always *listen*. I know that you cannot control what others are thinking. But even the fact that some people who have epilepsy feel comfortable enough to come to see me and talk to me about it, well, that is my little beacon of light.

I hang that light on my tree. I want my tree to give others hope, insight, and courage to persevere—even in the harshest conditions. Something in my energetic field helps people know that I am a safe person to talk to. When they come, they are added to my tree to become a forest. My family tree is a forest because of these companions and acquaintances.

So, friends of friends, or whoever has a question, usually regarding health, food, or design work, will call me. It usually starts with a chance meeting or someone telling them about me, and then that person randomly giving me a phone call or leaving a message.

It tends to go something like this: "Do you remember when we met going out to that baseball game with a bunch of other people from work? I have questions for you." A light bulb goes on in my head, and I just kind of smile to myself because I silently know that I am lending a helping hand. Those people finally understand it and want to know, and that is great to me! I either give them advice or ask them many questions to try to help them solve the problem. I might not always know exactly what I am doing to solve that problem, but I will figure it out most of the time!

Hands-on or exploring the options is my best bet! If you need help, let me know. I will come over, and we can do it together. Remember that no one is going to hold your hand or do it all for you. I cannot always be there for you. But with the information I give you, you will need to take responsibility for your own choices. I encourage you to ask a lot of questions and bring your responsibility. Everyone might not be my family, but let us all hang out and create our affirmations, our own family, and our happiness. You can create your future!

I will aid you in creating your forthcoming! I know that I am not always going to feel good internally. But, you cannot just sit there and be a pessimistic, gloomy, and depressed soul all of the time. I want that feeling of otherness, and my friends who are my own family. It is like you are a branch, a twig, a leaf that I add to my "family tree." I also see ghosts wandering around in my forest. They are never scary, but they are echoes of the past that bring hope to my trees.

Now I can pick my family and make the tree my own through the commonality with others. I just pretended I was something else in first grade, but now I know who I am and where I belong. I feel at peace with the beauty of nature and the trees surrounding me. Their grace intrigues me, from roots to leaves. I have always felt close to them, but a family tree without roots? How do you create the tree without those? So I just always consider everyone to be lineage. Even though they are not genetically bloodline, they seem to say to me,

"Oh, I will be your sister, or I will be your second mom." They get to come with me on my journey!

Imagine within the isolation of 2020, and I found out I had a second major health issue—all alone. I was dealing with another significant health concern—breast cancer. It was like I had received it from the heavens, and then someone clicked the button on the giant stopwatch called Earth.

Everything changed quite rapidly. I saw the whole hospital become quieter. And more things changed every day I came in. The only people allowed into the hospital were those with cancer or emergencies. I could not bring anyone supportive in with me anymore, and sometimes I would just have people drop me off. I was not even allowed to bring water into the building, even though I was constantly dehydrated. The water fountains were covered or completely turned off. Every waiting room was rearranged so that you could not wait or sit anywhere. Then I was escorted straight into a sanitized room by myself.

But then there was the other side of the solitude that gave me perspective and joy. I truly began to realize who my friends and other trees are. I did weekly Zoom sessions with allies, and relished doing more art again because I could not go anywhere. I took online classes that expanded my horizons. And I had more time to explore cooking, and experimented with working out more at home.

Identifying the Trees in Your Forest

Stick *Tree* *Forest*

How far do your branches reach when you choose how you want to live your personal life? I know that I am not going to wait until I retire. I never really believed too much in that statement. I am going to take time out for myself and embrace it. You might not ever get a chance to do that again—to enjoy life to the fullest and create your intrinsic wellness.

It is about taking charge and making choices in your life. For example, if you do not have a lot of money, get a second job or more clients, or change it somehow. For me, I love to travel. I put my desired destination on my calendar as a goal, and then I just make sure that I have enough money when that comes to me. I work and save up for it diligently. I have also learned that time moves quickly, and tomorrow will be here before you know it! If you plan something super unique that you want to do, you will save up for that even more! It is the power of positivity.

Overall, you cannot focus on the negatives. Some situations in my health will never change. But I always say to myself that *I DO NOT want to listen to that broken record!* The broken record is when I am listening to someone describe a lousy issue or negative situation. It usually reminds me of a past adverse circumstance. Everyone has problems to deal with, and some will just trap it inside and never deal with it at all, like a hole in your heart that never gets repaired. The past trauma will begin to swell up and make the pot boil over! But I also do not want others to feel sorry for me or throw a pity party.

Especially in the last few years of medical demands, I learned to take things one day, one problem, one medical issue at a time, so that I do not suffocate myself. On top of the woes of 2020, dealing with cancer is not something that I would wish on anyone. I would keep my mind moving forward, whether getting outside and taking a walk, or listening to some music that I love. That eagerness will thrust you into another realm of the living. So, take responsibility for creating your zeal, which can push you out of the negative and into your power.

The Root of the Tree

After forty years of searching, I recently found out who my birth father and birth mother are. About five years ago, I did a DNA test that helped explore traces of my tree bark. My family is content that I found my birth family, and others might not have the drive to do it, but my roots are slowly starting to form more and more into the truth. Some of these roots are not what I expected, but others are twofold! After creating this kingdom and making it how I wanted, then it hit me.

When reality sets in, it kind of spoils the fun. My ghost kingdom is not as glamorous anymore. The clouds are not as thick surrounding the castle, and the fog is slowly lifting. I never thought that ghosting was strange. But I felt like it is similar to when you are in a relationship, and you want to give it everything, but the other person does not.

I lived in this little area of mystery, and until I cleared off the outside of my glasses, I did not realize that they were taking advantage of me. It is weird now to see people that look like me. And trying to search for that lost kingdom, I never knew what to look for before, so I just never found it. Today, I am just trying to mend that curiosity and get used to the feeling of belonging, and knowing who I am.

And those gifts were given to me by my ghosts and the family and friends that I grew up with. Now I also know how two negatives can make a positive. Negative #1: Currently, the birth mother does not want to give me much information and is introverted. Negative #2: The birth father is very secluded in his own space and seems to ignore the truth. But when both of them are combined, BOOM! Cheerful: More family! I have great half-siblings, more new aunts and uncles, and then some!

An incredible gift was found through some of the ghost partners. I assume that my birth parents do not want to give me some information because of the shame, pain, or whatever their negativity has caused them. But this has left me with the most positive and amazing thing I have ever had. I connect with some kin and just enjoy this whole new ancestry that has opened to me!

So, have I always felt like an outsider? Not always. But I DO choose to create my zeal, and I try to empower others to take responsibility. If you do not try to do things that are not in your normal realm, you will never feel the excitement of the new ones! Try to fill in the blanks on your family tree, or figure out something you did not know yesterday! Meet someone new next time you go to the store, or even just do something different that will spice up your day a little bit!

The more sticks that you pick up will create enough wood for a beautiful tree. And the more trees that you find, the bigger the forest will be. Everyone will take their path in life. Create your forest, your own family, and your positives so that you can feel proud to know who you are. A place that *you* created so that you know that is where you belong.

For more information, feel free to contact me at:

nelsonswritingwell@gmail.com.

Chapter 6
Gifts From Sally
By Elaine Turso
Stubborn Pineal Clarifier

Do you remember having Pop Rocks candy as a kid? Pouring an entire pouch of what looked like colored Rice Krispies into your mouth, and it feels like something is exploding in your mouth? I remember we would all open our mouths so you could physically hear the crackling and fizzing that we were all experiencing. ADHD side note: Do you remember the urban legend that was made up about drinking soda and eating Pop Rocks? That Pop Rocks killed Mikey from the Life Cereal commercials? But I digress—back to the Pop Rocks.

Imagine these crackling and fizzing micro-explosions happening in your brain—all the time! You might call your intuitive voice something different, like squirrels, shiny objects, downloads, light bulb moments, brain dumps, random thoughts, etc. I call mine POP-ROCKS. They were out of control for a long time, and it has taken me a long time to learn how to rein them in.

Have you ever had a million-dollar Pop-Rock idea, but you don't listen or take action on it, and then discover someone else did it, and now has a billion -dollar company? And all you can say to yourself is, "Someone stole my idea!"

After you have said something to yourself, have you ever heard a response from the other side of your head after expressing something like that?

It's a strange experience, but I think all of us have.

I love going through my daily Facebook memories and seeing the random things I was going through over the years *on this day*. I have found multiple posts about million-dollar *ideas,* but I rarely shared the vision. Maybe I was afraid someone was going to steal it. But in my February 3, 2009 post, I shared my idea.

The post said: "I get these random ideas in my head. Today it was to open a clothing store with a twist. How many times do we say, 'I have nothing to wear.' So I thought it would be cool to be able to rent outfits before you buy them. And, of course, receive a consultation from a stylist. Then we could save money on buying new clothes."

Sound familiar? There's a top-rated clothing subscription service where you receive a stylist who sends you clothes to try on at home, keep what you like, and send back what you don't want. You know the one I'm talking about. According to my Google research, this company was founded in February, 2011 and is valued at 1.6 billion dollars. So, why didn't I pursue the idea?

Sally, my inner self-saboteur voice, would tell me that it was because I didn't have that kind of money. Money was always taking the blame or the big excuse for why I didn't follow through with any of my "brilliant, million-dollar, Pop-Rock ideas." In retrospect, I don't think it was about the money.

Who was I? I was a nobody. I was a property manager. I didn't belong in business! What experience did I have? Zero. I never even went to college (as if that was some prerequisite for being successful). I didn't have any professional certifications that would compel anyone with money to invest in launching this business idea when I had zero credentials and zero experience.

This company raised $120 million in its initial public offering (fancy business language) to get launched. In 2009, I was thirty-two years old, and all of my experience came from working in the low-income housing industry. So what would possess me to think that I could turn this into a successful business idea?

Sally was so great at keeping me from making a fool of myself.

THE GIFT OF VISIONS

In 2009, I started a side business of photography. After several years, I wanted to begin photographing women in "boudoir style." I knew that to understand how it would feel, I had to get in front of the camera. I had a photographer friend come to my house where I photographed her, and she photographed me. I needed to have the experience because I wanted to relate to how the clients would feel exposed and vulnerable. I watched my friend's confidence boost right in front of my eyes. I started to feel more confident in my skin too! That's when I fell in love with photographing women.

I discovered a new intuitive gift when I was photographing someone. I could close my eyes, and in the stillness, I would see a vision of how to pose them. One time, a client was a little confused about what I was doing, so I started explaining to people that I do this thing that might seem weird, but to just *trust me.*

We could be outside walking in the park, and suddenly, I would get this vision flash before my eyes, and I could visualize them doing a particular pose at a specific spot. Or, during a studio session where I was feeling out of ideas, I would close my eyes, and there it would come—the next Pop-Rock idea. Once I learned what they were and how to use them, my visions never failed me.

MEGA POP-ROCK

I felt like something was missing in my photography business. I couldn't quite put my finger on it, but something felt *off*. Here I was, photographing amazing, beautiful women, and they were feeling so insecure and unbeautiful. My pep talks were no longer cutting it. I wanted women to love themselves and see themselves the way the world saw them. I didn't understand why they weren't feeling how the world saw them.

I connected with a friend from New Mexico who has her intuitive gifts. I shared everything I was doing for these amazing women, but something felt like it was missing. She told me that I should coach women to build their confidence *before* their boudoir photoshoot. Interesting concept.

Guess what the first thing *Sally* said was?

"You are not qualified."

"You don't have any certifications."

"You don't have a degree."

"You are not a coach."

My friend challenged *Sally* for the first time about my belief that I had to have fancy degrees or certifications. I let her suggestion sit with me for a couple of days, and then all of a sudden, *it* happened.

While I was driving home, out of nowhere, I started getting an overwhelming rush of random names, song titles, phrases coming out in my thoughts. I didn't know what to do; this particular gift had never surfaced before. Since I was driving, I grabbed my phone and started using the "talk to text" feature to document the random stuff coming out of my brain. I was so afraid I was going to forget it. When I got home, I grabbed a notebook. I couldn't stop writing. I had to get every word out, even though it didn't make sense at the time.

I let the list marinade for a few days, and I added some additional thoughts as new Pop-Rocks came through. To make sense of these pages, I took all of this gibberish and organized it. I noticed a theme and was able to place each idea/phrase into four categories. As I counted all of them, I wound up with thirty topics. That's how the Perfectly Imperfect Body Image Boot Camp was born. Was this *Pop-Rock-of-an-idea* in alignment with my business? For the first time, YES!

Coaching women before they had a boudoir photo shoot was just what my clients needed, and it's just what I needed to set myself apart and stand out from every other photographer in my area.

Because I had never done this before, I decided to do a *beta* test of this program with four amazing women to validate this Pop-Rock idea.

What I didn't plan for was that the women would all form a community of support. I also didn't anticipate that I would have to confront my issues surrounding body image.

You see, when I was five years old, I suffered third-degree burns on my chest and arm. It impacted the way I viewed myself. I had built up this idea that I had to stay covered, to not draw attention to myself. I remember being in middle school and wearing a winter jacket zipped all the way up on a hot summer day. I tell you what, changing in the locker room after PE was my worst nightmare.

My first confrontation with body image came when my daughter was about nine years old. Imagine this sweet darling little girl telling you that she hates her thighs. Yeah, I know. Then imagine realizing that YOU were responsible for her feeling that way about her body. (F*&^#$ck!!!!!!). How could

I tell this sweet little adorable cheerleader that she should be happy that her thighs weren't as big as mine? (Double F*&k). P.S. That's my time machine moment. If Doc and Marty come to my house, I'm going back to that date so that I can change what the frick I said. Seriously. Whyyyyyyyyyyyyyyyyyy did I say that? Doc and Marty never did show up, but two other guys did—Guilt and Shame.

My first message of body positivity that changed my perspective came from an unexpected source: The Tyra Banks Show. I remember sitting on the couch and browsing channels and coming across her show with mothers and daughters. They were marking up silhouettes with X's on all the places on their body that they hated. They might as well have just put a giant X over the whole thing. It was awful and heartbreaking. How could these beautiful women and girls hate every inch of their bodies?

Their show psychologist (they always have one) said something that always stuck with me: "Daughters don't want to be better than their mothers." If I am unkind to my body, my daughter will be unkind to her body as well. So, all of the times that I said, "My fat ass won't fit in that chair" or "My thighs are too fat to wear leggings," I was telling my daughter that something was wrong with her body too. What in the holy F*&k have I done to my beautiful daughter? I was so angry at myself.

Think of going from guilt and shame to positivity and fame! I decided at that moment that I would immediately stop talking shit about myself. I had to, for her sake. I did something next that I was terrified to do, but was a critical step in my healing.

Let's pretend you are going to go skydiving. The night before you are about to jump out of an airplane, you are so nervous, and you probably start thinking of excuses why you should cancel. The butterflies are running rampant. You can barely sleep. All you can think about is the worst possible case scenario. All the bad things are running in your head.

You arrive at the drop zone. You feel like you want to vomit. Maybe you do, I don't know—I'm not there. You get training from the instructor. You remember nothing. Thank God they give you a tandem buddy because, Lord knows, you won't remember shit after jumping out of that perfect aircraft.

Here comes the moment. The doors open. You approach the deck, and all of a sudden you feel this rush of wind, and the pilot yells GOOOOOOOO! Your tandem buddy leans your body over the edge, and you have no choice but to jump.

Oh shit! You are freefalling out of the sky. There is screaming. There is cussing. There is pleading with your God. Then, for just a moment, you shut the hell up and realize that you are floating in the sky, and you get to see the world from a whole new perspective.

Suddenly, you get this rush of overwhelming feelings of gratitude. You begin to cry because you know your life will never be the same ever again. Your parachute opens, and you float down to the ground with the biggest smile on your face. The first words you say are, "Oh, my goodness, that was so fun. Let's do it again!"

When I compare leaving the house without a sweater for the first time to skydiving out of an airplane, you may think there is no way to reach the two things. Here's what's natural for me: I was scared to death. I wanted to vomit. Leaving the house in a spaghetti-strap baby-doll dress without my safety net, the sweater (aka the parachute), was a massive deal for me.

I decided that today was the day. I had heard Tyra Banks and her show talk about loving your body, and I was going to prove to my inner voice, *Sally*, that she was a liar. I had to convince myself that nobody was going to point, laugh or call me names. I walked out of the living room, and my husband had this stunned look on his face. He wasn't sure what to do or what to say. We were heading to the mall for the first time, where my scars would be visible to other human eyes. If I was going to show my daughter that I loved myself (and she should too), I had to do more than say it; I had to *live* it. I had to be the example—and I was scared as hell.

Guess what happened? Not a damn thing. No one gawked at me. No one pointed and laughed. No one screamed, "Freak!" *Sally* had lied to me. And I had at that moment taken back my power. She no longer had control over me. This became the moment that I treated *Sally* as my enemy. I had convinced myself that she did not have my best interest at heart, and my goal in life was to shut her mouth up.

Now, to tell you that I was automatically healed from this fear is frankly a crock of bullshit. I had proven that it could be done, but now I had to practice this newfound self-love every day. The real work would begin.

Here I am, several years later, a body-positive boudoir photographer and a want-to-be body-image coach, walking around telling everyone else to love themselves, and internally I was still struggling. Do you know what I worked with the most? This is going to sound silly, but it's the truth. I struggle with, and still to this day, I struggle with compliments/comments about my weight.

Truth bomb: When you realize that you gained back (and then some) all of the weight you lost because you didn't like people complimenting your weight loss. I sabotaged my health because I didn't like the attention I received. Whether it was a photo I posted on Facebook, or when I would see someone in person. The conversations of "You look amazing" or "Hey. skinny girl!" truly make me want to crawl up out of my skin and hide in the closet with my suitcase of Strawberry Shortcake dolls.

The Perfectly Imperfect Body Image Boot Camp (later named Getting Unf*$ked) would support women ready to heal from their pain, and start to change how I saw and felt about myself. The teacher was also the student.

Fun Fact: I seem to teach the things that I need to learn for myself. Can you relate to that?

PERMISSION TO CHANGE MY MIND

After ten years of photographing amazing, beautiful women, and experiencing almost two years of excruciating pain from sciatica, I was looking for permission from others to close my photography business. Because I couldn't, I wouldn't. I was looking for answers outside of *Sally*. Why? Because I didn't trust her. I didn't trust my intuition. I didn't believe in my abilities. I didn't have the confidence to start something new.

Would people accept me as anything other than a photographer? What would people think? What would they say? Would they be supportive? Would they think I was a quitter? Would they think of me as someone who starts something and doesn't finish it?

My entire sense of belonging had been wrapped up in my business. I had given myself all of these labels, and I had let others put them on me too. This was how I contributed to my family. Would I have to get a J-O-B? (P.S. I am a terrible employee, now that I've been an entrepreneur.)

I had an opportunity to attend a retreat on the beach in Oregon, and although I couldn't afford to go, I thought maybe I could get permission to quit while I was there.

Guess what? I didn't get permission to quit. Instead, I found myself confronting my fears around money. The fear of not sending my son to college was a significant source of 'stuck.' The fear of not contributing to my family without photography was a huge hurdle I had to face head-on.

Rather than getting permission to quit photography, I received some ideas around adding companion services, such as brainstorming, retreats, and other value-added services. Okay. Cool. I made a plan. I had received enough mojo to continue with my photography business. This meant that I would now be running *three* businesses *and* still running my local networking group.

I had been lightly dabbling in mentoring other entrepreneurs after discovering that I could use my Pop-Rocks to help others create their *million-dollar ideas*. I would connect with another entrepreneur and get this massive rush of thoughts and ideas when they talk about their business.

(I love it when people tell me that they can see my brain Pop-Rocking and that something extraordinary is about to happen.)

Do you know what sucks, though? When my brain comes up with a million-dollar Pop-Rock idea for someone else, and they don't implement a damn thing. At the time, I didn't realize that I could help them *implement* the idea. Even though I did not feel qualified, I began coaching, mentoring, and strategizing with other small business owners, even though I did not have fancy certifications. I had finally found my zone of genius.

Let me preface this next part with an analogy: Herding cats. Have you ever seen someone try to herd cats? Yeah, me neither. Because it's impossible! When I tell you that doing significant event group photography is equivalent to herding cats, you can hopefully feel my pain.

Have you ever experienced a wave of emotion come over you in a way that provides the most eye-opening clarity? Well, it happened to me when I was doing group photography. Suddenly, this wave came over me, and I remember distinctly thinking, "What in the hell are you doing? This does not bring you Joy." *Sally* was back. Except this time, I didn't shut her up, because she validated how I was already feeling.

This was the moment I had been waiting for. The moment I knew I was done.

Like when I had decided I was done photographing children, and with my car packed full of props, a client approached me asking me to photograph her toddler. The people pleaser, *Sally,* said yes, but doing the photo session helped me realize that I was making the right choice.

I knew it was over when I photographed a woman in my house that Monday following 'the wave,' and I felt like I was faking an orgasm—gross.

I knew I was done when I started a profanity subscription box, and it was not profitable after a year. As I was getting ready to design all the graphics for my Instagram grid, *Sally* came over to me like a wave and said: "Why are you spending so much time on something that is not profitable"? I was done, just like that.

I had to learn to permit myself to change my mind. Permission to let it go. Permission to change, evolve, grow, face the questions, and doubt—doubt from myself and doubt from the people who knew me.

I was learning to trust *Sally* again. I had to rely on that I was smart enough to make the right decisions. To confront and FACE my fears. Letting go of things that no longer brought me joy or were in my best interest has become so much easier. But the biggest thing that helped was having an honest conversation with my self-saboteur, *Sally*.

SELF-SABOTEUR SALLY

I was watching the newest season of "Atypical" on Netflix. Casey, the daughter, is a runner. Her dreams are to get accepted to UCLA on a track scholarship. She gets up every morning at 4:30 am. As my husband would say, she puts in the work. She finds out that a UCLA recruiter is attending her next track meet.

She sees her in the stands, and you can tell that she's letting the fear of success get to her. They all line up and get into their running stance, and the gun fires. Everyone takes off running, except Casey, who was frozen. She looks up and sees her parents yelling, "GO!" She stays frozen. Just standing there. Watching everyone else run, I imagine that she's thinking, "There's no way I can catch up now; I might as well just quit."

Living up to everyone's expectations can be paralyzing. When other people put their expectations on us, we are so afraid of letting them down.

When we are faced with our biggest fears, our choices are fight, flight, or freeze. In Casey's story, she froze. On the surface, Casey had everything going for her. A supportive family, a scholarship, everyone was on her side, rooting for her success.

The pressure of disappointing her parents, disappointing her school, disappointing her girlfriend became too much, and she sabotaged her success. I'm no stranger to the fear of disappointing others and letting that play a part in my decision-making process.

When I was a teenager, I skipped school with my best friend to spend the day with our boyfriends. We had timed everything perfectly. We left the house as if we were going to school. We would get home simultaneously, and I would erase the message on the answering machine from the school.

What I did not anticipate was that my mother would stay home sick from work that day. So she answered the phone and learned that I was not in school. She called my dad at work, and he was waiting for us as we crossed the bridge in the parking lot of the Godfather's Pizza. Standing with his arms crossed, leaning against his '67 red Impala, aka The Beast. I told my friend, "You have to sit in the front seat; I'm too scared." When we got to my house, her parents were also there. We were sooooooooo busted!

You see, I was the oldest of three, and the only girl. I got good grades. I was pretty quiet and tame. I had always been a rule follower. My dad said that one thing to me that makes every kid's heart fall to their stomach: "I'm not angry, I'm just disappointed."

That was the moment I learned that disappointing the people I loved and cared about didn't feel good, and I would do everything in my power to never disappoint anyone again—to my detriment.

Sally reminded me often that people couldn't be trusted, that no one would do it the way it should be done, and if pleasing others is on the table, you ought to just do it yourself. You don't want to look bad if others don't do their part of the project. Insert: *Over-achieving People-Pleaser Phoebe.* (She's another one of my inner voices.)

CONFRONTING SALLY

Imagine you are driving a car, and *Sally the Self-Saboteur* is trying to take over.

Knowing the history of her lying to me, I didn't want her driving the car and taking me to the wrong destination, and that's what I believed she would do.

I shoved her into the passenger seat because I had to be in control. I'm the driver. Then she starts messing with the radio, trying to put on country music, so I pull over the car and make her get in the back seat. Then she becomes the nagging back seat driver—telling me where to turn and when to signal. Just really being an annoying, sabotaging bitch. So, I pull over, and I forcefully put her ass in the trunk.

You see, I believed that to get to my destination, I couldn't listen to her. And I couldn't trust anyone else to help me. I believed that, to get shit done, I had to put her ass in the trunk and go at it alone. I truly believed that she was trying to prevent me from getting to my destination, when in fact, she was trying to warn me about the path ahead. She was trying to encourage me and show me a better way to get there.

I was conditioned to believe *Sally*, my inner voice, was trying to sabotage my success. It wasn't until I was writing this chapter of this book that I realized that I treated *Sally* as my enemy this entire time. I treated her as the bitch that needed to be silenced, and my metaphor to do that was to put her ass in the trunk. I always acknowledged that she was trying to keep me safe, but I never acknowledged that she was trying to *HELP* me and not *HURT* me.

Sally was with me when I started my scrapbooking business.
She was with me when I started my photography business.

She was with me when I moved my studio to a new location.

She was with me when I launched a chapter of Polka Dot Powerhouse.

She was with me when I wrote my first book.

She was with me when I launched a subscription box.

She was with me when I permitted myself to let go of the photography business and move into business coaching.

She was with me when I permitted myself to let go of the subscription box.

She was with me when I launched my new marketing agency.

She was with me when I permitted myself to let go of my local Polka Dot Powerhouse chapter.

She has been gently tapping me on the shoulder and guiding me this whole time. Now I can see that she has been guiding me along the way and coming through in various inner voices, because she knew I wouldn't listen to her.

If hindsight were 20/20, I could tell you that the reason my first million-dollar *Pop-Rock idea* didn't come to fruition was that it wasn't in alignment for me. *Sally* was there to tell me that this was not my path. *This idea didn't belong to me.* She wasn't telling me that I wasn't good enough or that it was a dumb idea; she said to me that the idea wasn't meant for me. It wasn't in alignment.

This lesson has helped me recognize which ideas were intended for me, or for someone else I know. It's not uncommon for me to get Pop-Rocks for someone, days after we have spoken.

SELF-SABOTEUR SALLY becomes STRAIGHT-TALK SALLY

Now that Sally and I have agreed, I know that I can count on her to be straight with me. I now know that she is not here to hurt me, but to help me. To be honest, to give it to me straight. Her job is to ask me hard questions and make sure that I am always in alignment. To keep those million-dollar Pop-Rocks in check. Asking me, "Are you sure this idea is in alignment for you? Is this a million-dollar idea for you, or is it for someone else?"

And that's something I can now appreciate about her. Thank you, Sally.

So, the next time, you start to hear that inner voice that lives deep within, instead of assuming that its purpose is to cause you harm, ask if the idea is in alignment with your dreams, values, and goals. You might be surprised to hear what she has to say.

Chapter 7
One Starfish at a Time
By Angela Witczak
Angry Thyroid Manifestor

Have you ever had someone say something so vile to you that questions your entire existence? For me, it started with a letter—well, two. The first was a letter sent to me by another person, or maybe even a group of people. I will never know, as the letter was purposely left unsigned. The second letter was also written to me, but the author was someone I knew. Someone I cherished. Someone I trusted. Both of these letters would change the very direction of my life, even though I didn't realize it at the moment.

The first letter came to me in the middle of the week on a beautiful afternoon. It was in a standard-size envelope with my name typed on the front. No return address made me curious and excited all at the same time. I love getting mail. The more letters, the better—just no bills, please. As I opened the mail, I was standing at the kitchen counter joking with my husband about something we had done earlier that day.

I tore open the envelope, and there was a typed letter with my name on the top. At first, I giggled, still in a joking manner with my husband, thinking to myself, *this is probably one of those old chain letters finally catching up to me. I am going to be so annoyed if someone sent me that.* But then, I started to read the words, and the rest of my body completely stopped moving.

I just stood there in my kitchen, with my eyes reading as fast as my brain could process the words —disgusting, vile, and accusatory words. My skin was crawling with a hot, icy sensation, and I was becoming nauseous. Someone had sent me a two-page letter that was filled with hate, and there was nothing for me to do but just stand there looking dumbfounded. I could taste the uprising bile in my mouth.

I flipped to the second page, desperately looking for a signature—nothing but a hollow space. The speed that I consumed the vile words seemed to come at me like daggers. Each word I read would tear at my heart and shred my soul. I pulled my eyes back away from the words and searched in vain, again and again, at that empty space on the back of the page. I didn't even have a clue as to who would have sent me such a letter. I read and reread it over the next few minutes, searching the words for any sort of indication of how to solve this awful mystery.

I felt crazy for a moment. You know when someone says something so awful to you, and your brain cannot even comprehend the severity of what was said, and the physical impact it does on your soul, so you just shut down completely? That was happening to me. The room was spinning around me. I began to question what I thought about myself, and even more so, what others thought of me.

Why? Why was I tearing myself down? I had to stop and take a breath. In, two, three, four, and out, two, three, four, I repeated until I could pull up my semi-normal brain and start better self-talk. Ok, I thought, "I know who I am. I am Angela, and I am amazing." my brain began. You see, I had spent six years working on myself after my second divorce. I paid thousands of dollars to seminars, workshops, therapists, and coaches. I had done the work to be a better woman. But then, this—out of the complete blue? This crazy piece of hate mail didn't bring me any sort of positivity—only negativity. So I grabbed my coaching skills and continued to remind myself of who I actually am.

I looked down at the letter in my hand, and my brain, with oxygen again, brought me back to one of the workshops I had attended a few years ago. I had spent the weekend working on myself—digging deep into my soul, searching for answers. I wanted a life-altering change, but didn't know how to get there. The weekend was filled with exercises and experiences designed to make people question their lives and bring awareness to possibility.

At the end of the weekend, I was standing in a circle holding hands with the rest of the people from the workshop, who had become like family to me. The workshop facilitator in the middle of the circle was relaying two stories. I didn't know it then, but these two stories were much like my two letters. The first story was about a bucket of crabs.

Did you know that if you put a bunch of crabs into a bucket, you don't have to put a lid on it? The crabs will never escape because as one crab gets to the top of the bucket to get out, the other crabs will pull it back down. Negativity works the same way. Have you ever noticed how the more successful you are, the more the haters will come out of the woodwork to pull you down?

The more I reread the words written to me, the more anger I felt. What had I done to make this person hate me so, and why was I the target of their affliction? I sat with that letter for days; bitter, angry, and sad. I felt my inner shine and dazzle feel dull and broken. It was as if the air had been sucked from my body, and I no longer knew what I was supposed to do with the rest of my life.

I eventually threw the letter away, but the words remained etched on my heart like a bad tattoo. You know, the kind of tattoo you get done while in college and have had one too many beers, and your sister's boyfriend is an aspiring tattoo artist. It was like that. I was deflated, but because I have such a great group of friends and coaches in my life, I could at least put one foot in front of the other. I shook off my pain and anguish. At least, I pretended to mask it well and went on with myself.

A few weeks after receiving this piece of hate mail, I was attending a new personal growth seminar. This workshop was based on abundance. Ever since my second divorce, I had been learning about ways to change my life. I never wanted to live the way I had been before my rock bottom experience (of divorce), so I constantly worked on improving myself.

While I was there, we were asked to write down our most significant and deepest desires. We were instructed to write a short letter to ourselves. What did we want most in our life, our number one goal? We had time to think, time to hold space, meditate, and pray. Whatever we needed, we could have at that moment as we thought about our life.

In the back of my head, I was instantly judging myself. Nothing I was going to write down would be good enough. The words of hatred were winning over me. I wasn't a good enough person to have dreams like the presenter was asking. *I am never going to make a difference in this world*, which is what I desperately desired. The more I sat there, the more I went back and forth with what I wanted.

I lived in poverty most of my life, and finally was at a place to change that. I had finally just started cracking open my soul to be open to a different way of thinking, only to have it shut down by words from a villain. And so there I sat, wondering if I could even dare to dream something so big.

I wrote down my main goal: *Giving away a million dollars to charities and churches, and paying it forward by June 2nd, 2040.* After I wrote it down, I thought about what I was writing. What were the parameters? Did I mean that I had to give a million dollars away personally, or could it simply mean that I was a facilitator in the process of raising a million dollars?

That was it! That was my biggest goal and letter to myself. I could manifest money for organizations that were near and dear to me. But even though I wasn't personally going to give a million dollars out of my pocket, that dream still felt so far out of reach.

As I sat in that chair, I started doing the math in my head and thought I was completely crazy. First of all, I would have to raise $40,000 a year consecutively for the next 25 years. Secondly, my annual income wasn't even $40,000 a year! *Who was I to think that people would even give me money!* While I was a somewhat active member of my community, I was also "uneducated and too loud for my own good." I often didn't fit in with the community leaders. I wasn't born and raised in the community I lived in, and I often felt outside most influencers. It was a lofty and insane goal, but I wanted to beat the demon voices in my head and make a difference in this world.

I went home from that weekend feeling high on life. Whenever I better myself, I get this deep sense of growth and excitement and feel wholly charged up to do anything. The three-hour drive back to my house was filled with empowering music blasted at total volume, with me singing badly at the top of my lungs. I felt great, on top of the world even!

And then I walked through the front doors of my house. It had been raining while I was gone, and my roof always leaked when it rained. There were pots and pans scattered through my living room and kitchen, and my husband was trying to find more towels.

Ugh, this again? The high that I had just been riding brought me back down to reality. How could I be anything in this world when, obviously, I couldn't even afford a new roof? I couldn't even take care of basic needs like "proper shelter" when I wanted to raise thousands of dollars for others. What kind of difference could I even make when this was my reality on a day-to-day basis.

I walked up to my bedroom to drop my suitcase after my trip. My heart was mixed up with all of these feelings of joy and sadness. I made my way into the bathroom, and there was my little secret room. The master bedroom in my house had a room, four closets, and a large bathroom attached to it. Three of the closets were standard-sized, while one was an extra-large walk-in closet.

Because we (my new husband and I) had seven of our eight kids still living at home, space was an absolute commodity. I needed a little place to get away from everyone, so my husband let me turn the walk-in closet into an "office." My office was about three-and-a-half feet wide and four feet deep. It was just big enough for me to put an old leather chair I had found at a thrift store in it, along with a petite table for my computer. I hung pictures of all of my favorite things on the walls—photos of my family and friends, the circus, random postcards, and one picture of a starfish.

When I was walking past my little closet-office, my eyes lingered on the pictures. I could hear the rain pouring down on my roof overhead and the water dripping in the walls. I closed my eyes, drew a deep breath through gritted teeth, and blew the air back out of my mouth, forcefully. I opened my eyes and looked around, when I was drawn to the starfish picture.

I had almost forgotten about the story of the starfish. At that same personal growth conference where I had heard about the story of the crabs, I had listened to another account.

The story of the starfish goes a bit like this:

An old lady was walking down the beach when she noticed the sand was covered in starfish. Hundreds, maybe thousands, had washed up on the beach with the receding of the tides. Up ahead was a small girl. The older woman noticed that occasionally the small girl would bend down, pick something up and throw it into the ocean. She quickly understood that the little girl was trying to throw the starfish into the sea.

The woman yelled out to the girl, "There are too many! You can never make a difference!" The little girl just stood there and thought for a moment. She then looked back at the old lady and then down at the starfish. Slowly, while deep in thought, she crouched down to the ground where she had been standing and then picked up another starfish and threw it into the sea. She yelled back to the woman, "Well, I made a difference to that one!" And then she turned and continued on her way, saving one starfish at a time.

I stood there in my little office just looking at that picture I had hung—a sole picture of a starfish that I had found on the clearance rack after I came home from that very first conference I attended. That story had been so impactful to me; I had wanted a reminder so I might never forget how important it was to make a difference, even if that difference was just one person at a time.

I stood there looking at that picture, and a huge smile filled my face. I knew I could make a difference. I thought back to all the times in my life that I had raised money or been associated with a charity of some sort. The more I thought about it, the more I realized that being a giver was ingrained in me, like an impression of an old fossil.

The first time I wanted to make a difference in the world I was six years old. I entered a coloring contest for a statewide seatbelt campaign in the 1980s. Back in those days, children wearing seatbelts was a new idea, and there was a company that wanted to raise money and awareness to create change. I drew a poster with a baby in a car seat, with the caption that said, "Is your child's life worth an extra 30 seconds?" My sign won the campaign at my school, and I received an honorable mention statewide.

That was my first taste of making a difference, even if it was minimal. Growing up, I found myself becoming impassioned with life's causes. I went door to door for a month asking for donations for a local bikeathon where we were working to end child abuse. I rode 20 miles on my broken-down Schwinn bike on a hot summer day, but I had raised over $500 for the cause. I still remember pushing my bike up a massive hill on a back road in Minnesota when an older boy came up to me and said, "Wow, good job, kid. You raised more than all of us." My heart swelled with pride.

When I was thirteen years old, my life took a turn in the middle of the 8th grade. My parents moved from that small town in Minnesota, closer to family in Wisconsin. I became bitter and angry, and started to look out for myself. I still cared about many causes - the poor, needy, and oppressed - but I was often jaded to the world around me. I began to believe that the world didn't need me to change it, or at the very least, I was unable to change it.

I continued to raise money for different causes and events throughout high school and my young adult life, but at the same time, I felt broken. I wasn't wealthy. I didn't come from an influential family. I had no college education, and so simply put, I felt like a dumb girl from a small town. The older I got, the more I became embittered about the injustice of the world. It was like living a double life -- wanting to raise money for others but constantly being so broke myself.

After a while, my zest for life began to dull, and I could barely keep food on my table, let alone help others. I was the one that needed saving. The harder I tried to pull myself out of the despair, the further I sank in. I made one wrong choice after another until I found myself battered and bruised after my second divorce, with nowhere to go but up.

And that is where I chose to change. I learned that the only way I could have something different in my life was to go after it myself. I had the power within me! No one else could take away my passion or steal my joy; that was for me to decide.

And so, I went to seminars, where there were millionaires who reminded me that life was a choice. People who told me stories of overcoming the worst of situations. Even though I sat there listening, feeling like an utter fraud, I truly believed that if they could do it, so could I.

I traded in my negative way of thinking, bitterness, and anger, and started living with joy on a day-to-day basis. I learned the power of forgiveness and how to overcome obstacles that were standing in my way. I found freedom in my life, knowing that I could change.

One of the speakers at the seminars said: "If you find yourself saying *'Someone ought to do something about that,'* take a look in the mirror, because you are someone." I thought long and hard about those words; later, they would become my life's mantra.

But I was only one person. What could I do even to make a difference? And then, again, I remembered the starfish story, that I could make a difference, just one person at a time. And that is how it began for me. For years, I got involved with committees, charities, small fundraisers, and even galas. I would help groups with big ideas that would bring in some money, and then I would go on to the next thing.

I was amid these smaller fundraisers when I received these two letters. The two letters would change my way of thinking. After coming home from the abundance workshop and seeing the starfish on my wall, I knew I needed to step into my greatness. I knew that I needed to be the one to look in the mirror and figure out what I could do, how I could be the one to help.

And so, I simply looked around my community. What was one thing I could do to help? The answers came flooding in. We needed new parks. Our community no longer had a Fourth of July celebration. We required more family-friendly ideas for New Year's Eve, and on and on, the pictures came in. And I became a part of them all. I found myself thriving for the first time in years. I had found my spot in my community. I finally felt like I belonged somewhere.

The first year after I wrote that letter to myself, I raised about $20k for different charities and organizations. I sat down and evaluated what I was doing right and what I could do better. I went on to question everything about my life. *Who did I think I was, trying something so grand in nature with no wealth, prestige, or education to back it up?* But the answer always came back to me in the form of the starfish. I could make a difference one person at a time.

In early 2019, I had been sitting on three different committees at the time. It was precious work, and I was thrilled with where my life was heading. I was running a full-time company, and I was a wife and mother. My life seemed like it was complete. I was even overflowing! But something was still missing, my heart still had gaps to fill, and I was a long way off of my fundraising goals.

I wanted to be a part of something that made a difference, a real difference. One afternoon, someone on Facebook posted about a homeless man who was sleeping in the town square. There were comments about "why the city doesn't do something about the white trash that lines our streets." I was furious. The city where I lived was cutely branded *The Greatest Place on Earth,* and yet here we had homeless in our streets, but no shelter to house them. Our community had once had a warming shelter for the winter months, but it had since closed, due to a lack of funding.

I went on a Facebook tirade about how frustrated and angry I was due to the lack of care and compassion our city was showing to the least of these in our neighborhoods. *Wasn't there anyone that could help? Who were we to judge this man's situation? How can we help him?* I cried and pleaded with the land of Facebook.

Someone from a brand-new committee saw my rant and reached out to me. A group of individuals was forming a new nonprofit to create a homeless shelter in our community. There was an offer from a church that we could move in immediately if the local municipality would agree to it.

I was unsure how involved I wanted to get in that project. On the one hand, my heart felt like I was called to be a part of this project, as there had been a few times I had been near homelessness myself. On the other hand, I felt like a total fraud. My husband and I were living paycheck to paycheck, my roof was caving in, and I was trying to keep my life together.

However, the meeting I went to at the local city hall solidified what I needed to do. There had been an open discussion about whether the village would allow a homeless shelter in the local church, and whether they would be willing to change the permit to allow for it. An angry mob of naysayers spoke against *those sort of people*, which broke my heart. I was one of the many to speak in favor of having a shelter come to our city.

Our little town of 12,000 people had an average of eighty-two homeless people and families sleeping on our streets. A study in our community found that the average age of homelessness was just nine years old. Being a mother, and knowing how close I had come to almost being a statistic, my heart was in shambles. I gave my three-minute comment to speak in favor of the church becoming a shelter. The village president looked straight into my eyes and told me that he was not interested in sacrificing his park (located across the street), that he worked so hard to build, for local junkies and criminals who would come through and destroy it.

My heart broke that night, and I knew that I had to be a part of this project over any other project in my community. With everything in my being, I knew that we had to help these men, women, and children break their chains of poverty and help create a new life for them. I was driven for change.

I started attending every village meeting they had on the topic, and eventually, the village formally decided not to allow the shelter to be built. The blood in my body boiled red hot with anger, hurt, and sadness for the people who would go to bed that night, once again without a bed. I couldn't understand how community members would let other members of their same community not have a place to lay their heads at night. I couldn't understand why they would rather see them freeze to death in their cars than allow them sanctuary in a local church.

A few weeks after the final decision was made, I received a call from the non-profit board president. There was a new 3-year term opening on the board; I didn't hesitate. I knew, without a shadow of a doubt, that I needed to be a part of this project. I gave him a firm *YES,* without so much as a second thought.

I knew that I needed to be a part of this change. I was tired of waiting around for someone else to do something, and I decided that someone was to be me. After just two months on the committee, our organization found a new building for our shelter. Somewhere that would end up even better than our original choice. The problem, however, was money. We were going to need a lot of money to make the changes. We would have to start basically from scratch.

We were given the opportunity to rent an old nursing home. The facility layout was already set up to have rooms, a kitchen, and even showers. Because of the new layout, we would be able to house men, women, and children in the same building, which we hadn't initially considered a possibility. The building had been vandalized and required a lot of repairs. And repairs required money—a LOT of money.

I knew what I needed to do. I got to work. I called everyone I knew. I helped create events, drives, and fundraising days at local restaurants. I reached out to businesses and asked for large sums of money. I was shameless when it came to this cause. And that's where I found my sparkle, my shine, and my passion. I finally remembered who I was.

I had always known I was pretty successful when it came to raising money, but I often didn't believe in myself enough. I thought the only way for someone to hand me a check with multiple zeros on it meant that I needed some sort of degree or accreditation, or had my life together more. I was so wrong. The only thing I needed was to be my authentic self. To have a heart for those who needed to have someone help make a difference.

In less than a year, we raised over $250,000. That put me well over a quarter of the way to my million-dollar goal, and my heart swelled with joy. After major renovations to our building, our shelter was finally opened, and now we can serve 32 clients at a time. We are the first shelter in a five-county radius that can house men, women, and children at the same time. Since we opened, I have seen miracle after miracle happen.

Our shelter was opened in the middle of a world crisis when people were at their lowest. And yet, there we were helping them. Our shelter is so much more than just a place for people to lay their heads at night and receive a warm meal. After a lot of work during the building process, we wanted to create something other shelters were not doing. We wanted our clients to gain skills, knowledge, and a pathway to break the chains of homelessness. We wanted to offer something that would help impoverished people access something more, and give them something to believe in: the ability to change their life, one step at a time.

I was recently chatting with a member of our community who has been a massive supporter of the shelter. She admitted to me that she needed some help from one of our organization's programs. She told me how ashamed she felt of asking for help when she has also been the one to help others. While she was talking, I sat there with a smile and waited for her to finish.

I sat there thinking about my roof that had been leaking for years. The roof I had only just recently gotten fixed. I still listen for dripping water every time it rains. "Just because you need help does not mean you cannot also be a helper! Look at the difference you made to all those people who needed you at the shelter!" Even as the words came out of my mouth, I was taken back to the starfish story.

I think about that little girl on the beach, with a heart like mine. And I would like to believe there is more to the story, and I have considered this. Once that sweet little girl realized how she was only one person, she left the beach. The old woman stood smugly and thought to herself, "See, I was right, there were too many starfish. The whole thing was useless." But then, moments later, she heard a rumbling of voices. The woman saw the young girl coming back over the sand dune with an army of friends. Children, big and small, came to save starfish. Each one making a difference in their way.

I have thought a lot about that little starfish story and the letters that I have received. I could have let both letters defeat me. The one filled with vile could have torn me to pieces. I could have chosen to give up altogether and not do anything, or become anything. The second letter also could have defeated me. I could have let the enormous nature of the goal overtake me. I could have given up on helping others because my own life was filled with struggle.

The fact is, I made a conscious choice that I would help people, one person at a time. I found through the years that I did not need to have my whole life together to help another person. I was simply required only to be one step ahead of the person behind me, so I could reach back and help the next person up as well.

As sick and twisted as it may feel, I had to give thanks to the people who pushed me to do better, even if that meant being on the receiving end of hatred. And not only that, I learned an even more significant and more valuable lesson of love, hope, and forgiveness. You see, that little girl had first to forgive that woman and not lose hope, so she could continue to show great love to the rest of the world.

I learned that little girl was me. That little girl had been inside of me for so long, and she was only waiting for the right time to come out. When that little girl (me) truly learned that she could lock arms with others around her, she was able to discover greatness.

I thought the goal I made in 2017 would be unattainable. I felt that way because I set limits, boundaries, and roadblocks in my way, believing that I could *never* achieve such a thing when I held myself back by my insecurities.

When I finally got out of my way and just took the next step in my life, I quickly learned I could create magic around me. My lofty goal of giving a million dollars away over twenty years suddenly became a reality. In fact, at the time of this writing, I have raised well over $750,000 for local charities, organizations, and events in my community, in just five years, not 25 years like I initially thought. I have been a part of new parks, scholarships for children, celebrations, events, and my beloved homeless shelter, where lives are being changed every day—one person at a time.

Not only that, but I now help organizations and individuals find ways to create funding for their passion projects. So many of us have needed permission to let that little girl out and make a difference, and I do just that. I remind women that they are valuable and loved. It's easy to lose hope when the world feels dismal with a leaky roof, a crying baby, and feeling worthless each day. But I assure you that there is still hope!

Let me leave you with this. I have learned the depths of forgiveness. I have learned how to love deeper from my experience working with the homeless and with women of all backgrounds. I have attended personal growth seminars, and when listening to keynote speakers, I found answers to prayers that I had in my heart. And since being an active member of my community, I have discovered that the needs of others are far more significant than my own, and I can still make a difference.

As I work on each project, I see myself putting the starfish down and whispering to it, "I'll be right back," and with purpose, I walk over the sand-dune, find/gather my people, return to the beach, and pick up my starfish, whispering, "We are here for you!"

This is love, and now I live in a great space of generosity. But perhaps the greatest lesson of my life comes from a tiny ocean animal, the starfish. I don't need to have my whole life together; I simply need to make a difference—

one step and one person at a time.

Chapter 8
You Won't Boil Me Alive

By Keely Crook
Emotional Pituitary Contributor

I wiped the fog from the bathroom mirror, took a deep breath, and exhaled. I looked at my eyes and thought about how tired I looked. I proceeded to get dressed in my room and turned on some music. Katy Perry's song, "Rise," was playing. I thought about how this song had helped me through the process of leaving my ex-husband. In the video for the song, Katy Perry is ridiculously dragging a parachute around the entire time. There are outside forces to navigate, the harsh desert, rain, a pool of water, and jagged cliffs. She could have unhooked herself and walked away at any time, but she kept dragging the parachute around like an anchor.

At one point in the video, it almost drowns her. I completely related to seeing her struggle through this pain and not knowing how to fix it. In the end, she had the power to improve her situation all along. I think that is why I liked the video so much. The lyrics were powerful and helped reinforce that I needed the strength to get through my experience.

I finished putting on jeans and a t-shirt and thought about this casual interview. What would I say? Should I be completely vulnerable? Tell everything as I experienced it and be honest? Or should I sugarcoat my answers? Ugh. I was overthinking this.

Barefoot, I went downstairs and made some coffee in the kitchen. I realized that I wasn't nervous about the interview but was worried about possible repercussions and reactions to my answers. "Walking on eggshells" had become a way of life for me in my past, and I told myself that not walking on eggshells was the only way to change patterns and my future. My experience had also taught me that I didn't need outside validation. I had learned to start trusting myself again, which confirmed that the only validation I needed was my own.

Again, I took a deep breath and exhaled as I walked into the living room with my freshly brewed coffee. My coffee cup had a picture of Wonder Woman on it that said, "As lovely as Aphrodite. As wise as Athena." My coffee mug reminded me of another song that had helped me rise above—the song "Unstoppable," by Sia. There was a video a fan had made of this song to the Wonder Woman movie. As silly as it sounds, I imagined the bullets and bombs she deflected with her shield and arm cuffs were insults, putdowns, belittling, yelling, and name-calling. I imagined all these things ricocheting off me as though I was made of steel.

I sat down on the couch and prepared myself to answer some tough questions. I thought to myself, "It'll be ok...I can do this." I hoped that my story would help someone else. Even if it only reached ONE person and they found hope, strength, or guidance from it, I would have served my purpose for doing this interview. I was ready.

The interviewer had kind green eyes and a soft smile. I felt instantly comfortable and at ease in her presence. She felt like an old friend I hadn't seen in a while. I looked up at the clock, back at my coffee, took a deep breath, and looked back into her green eyes. I was ready for her questions. She plunged right in.

Good morning! I hope you are doing well today. Thanks so much for sitting down with me and talking through your experience. I know this isn't easy for you. To start, would you mind sharing a bit of your situation and the progression of things with me?

Thank you. My story isn't easy to talk about. It's mostly because I feel naive, and it makes me feel weak and very unintelligent. I am afraid that people will read this interview and think, "How did she not understand what was happening?" Or "Why didn't she just leave him right away?" But things just weren't that simple. I genuinely hope that this helps someone out there who finds themselves in a similar situation.

Thank you for stating that. How would you describe what happened to you?

Well, I was pursuing my dreams, being a mom, all the while navigating my way through an abusive relationship. What I experienced with Brad didn't occur overnight. Let me be clear. It happened over six years, but progressively got worse. Incidents would occur that would be followed by periods of calm. Then another incident and a period of peace. After these incidents would happen, I'd suffer from a bit of amnesia—clinging to a false hope that things would get better. There is a book that I will refer to later, but the author provides an example of a frog being boiled alive. Have you ever heard of that?

Yes, I think I have. It depicts a frog being boiled alive, slowly over time. The frog is initially placed into a large pot with tepid water. The heat of the water gradually increases, so the frog acclimates to the higher temperatures.

Eventually, the frog boils alive without it ever attempting to jump out of the pot. If the frog were placed into hot water from the start, it would immediately jump out of the pot, fully aware of the present danger. Did I get the story right?

Yes! That's the story, and Brad's behavior toward me heated up slowly over time.

Would you mind sharing with me what you were like before you met Brad?

Before I met Brad, I viewed myself as a whole person, not someone searching for a missing piece. Just two years earlier, I had trained for and competed in a bodybuilding competition. I used a combination of life experience, research and found a book that helped me navigate my workouts. I had only enlisted the help of a trainer eight weeks before my competition to safely help me with my diet and exercises leading up to the event.

Part of how I operate and who I am entails doing research and completely immersing myself in a goal. My hobbies involve reading multiple books (all at once), absorbing information, taking notes, forming a plan, and acting on this information I've collected. Sometimes I don't even have all the information and find myself picking up puzzle pieces and putting them together as I go.

Learning and growing are what make me feel alive! When I am pursuing something new, I make connections with people who have accomplished what I was researching or wanted to do. Sometimes these connections were temporary, and other times, they turned out to be critical connections that altered the direction of my life. You just never know when you meet someone how they might impact your future! That is why I always do my best to leave things on good terms, whether it is a relationship, job, or friendship. I am also honest to a fault. Sometimes I can be a little too blunt about things, but I do my very best to be discreet and respectful.

My life leading up to Brad had been filled with examples of me learning something new, or accomplishing something someone else didn't think I could. I do not pursue things for the sole purpose of proving someone wrong. However, I firmly believe it's wrong to define another person. How do you know what someone else is capable of? Unless you live inside that person's mind—you'll never know that answer.

It sounds like you didn't need a relationship, but wanted to be with the right person who would add happiness to your life.

Absolutely! I was looking for a partner who wanted to contribute as much to the relationship as I did! Equal give and take. However, I realize that relationships aren't perfect, and at times one partner will sometimes give more than the other. In my mind, a relationship should mutually *feel* fair to both people. If the scale is tipped too far to one side, they should openly discuss any issues and find solutions that bring the relationship back to equilibrium for both partners.

How did you meet Brad?

I met Brad online. I was in search of someone who lived close to me. However, being so busy myself, a long-distance relationship seemed appealing because I could maintain my everyday life, friends, family and take things slow! Brad happened to be in the state, but far enough away I wouldn't see him every day.

When did you first notice anything wrong?

Well, at the beginning of any relationship, things were perfect! Brad made me laugh! He had a great sense of humor, told corny jokes, and poked fun at me in a playful way. We both enjoyed the outdoors, listened to similar music, loved to travel, and shared similar views on religion, sex, politics, and money. It seemed like Fate!

We were both into personal growth, and I liked the idea of growing old with someone throughout life. It seemed like we shared a mutual understanding of how change and development were significant in a relationship. However, after dating for six months, he started looking through my mail. He confronted me about a loan I had, and the way he had asked me about it had made me feel uncomfortable—like he didn't trust me.

It's like he was accusing me of wrongdoing, and I felt the need to apologize even though I hadn't done anything wrong. I didn't even think about asking him about HIS debts or why he looked through my open mail. He said he couldn't live with or marry someone who had money trouble and that he needed reassurance that I wasn't in over my head. I assured him I was paying my debts fine and that I wasn't in any financial trouble. I found out later from my friends that he had even asked THEM about my finances!

It sounds like he was breaching some boundaries there! How did that make you feel?

I've thought so much about things afterward. I realize now that when my boundaries were being pushed, I would experience an overwhelming feeling of being caught off guard, shocked, confused, and demeaned. When this happened, I would often find myself giving in, apologizing, or trying to explain myself in situations where I didn't need to.

The example I gave you about him snooping through my mail and interrogating me is one instance. I really should have been questioning why he was looking through *my* mail without *my* permission. *Spying* was a breach of trust! Had I listened to my feelings, I would have understood that he had crossed a boundary. This was when the water in the *frog pot* started getting a little warmer.

Were there other red flags you noticed in your relationship?

Occasionally. And again, we would get into fights about things, like any average couple. One thing that did confuse me was how the arguments seemed to be over something that bothered him about me. Being a single mom and working full time, sometimes I was too exhausted to keep the house completely organized. If Brad came over and it wasn't as tidy as his place, he'd act disappointed or become a bit upset. He'd say things to me that insinuated if I didn't keep my place tidy enough, maybe we shouldn't move in together.

I remember feeling confused and hurt after he'd say things like this. I had a feeling like I wasn't good enough. Maybe there was something wrong with me? How could I be a single mom with ONE kid and not keep my place super tidy? I mean, Brad had even told me how he had dated some other lady who had four kids once, and she had kept her place spotless! I tried to be better about it and made sure nothing was out of order before Brad would visit me.

Sometimes I'd feel a little sick to my stomach before he'd show up, worried that I missed something, and that he'd point it out and be disappointed or angry with me. Had I listened to my feelings, I understood that Brad was putting me down and unfairly comparing me to others. I had allowed him to cross another boundary.

So, when you say you "allowed him to cross another boundary," what do you mean by that?

Part of a healthy relationship is having healthy boundaries and being able to communicate what they are. Sadly, I didn't learn this early on in my life, and it took meeting Brad to understand this about myself. Not understanding my boundaries caused me to ignore my feelings and allow other people to dictate how I should feel about things. One example of this would be when you see a child fall and the parents say, "Oh, you're ok, stop crying." The parents may be well-meaning, but to the child, they are creating a different reality that says, "You didn't fall. You aren't hurt, so the pain you are feeling right now isn't real."

The better way to handle the situation might be to ask the child, "Are you okay?" That example may sound ridiculous, but the point is to see the problem from someone else's perspective. People feel pain in varying intensities. Over time, because I was denied having my feelings or expressing my own emotions growing up, I often couldn't understand when people were crossing a boundary. Instead, I was left with a sense of confusion, hurt, or anger. I would know something was *off* but couldn't correctly identify the problem or address it effectively.

I think I need to reassess my childhood! I can understand what you're saying. Our parents grew up with patterns from their parents, and it just gets passed to future generations. Do you recall anything that bothered you about Brad?

Hmmm. Weirdly, nothing bothered me about Brad at the time. I guess I was so worried about pleasing him that I didn't see how things were going in the wrong direction from the beginning. He had a way of deflecting things and turning them around on me. For example, if I got upset at him about arriving late to pick me up, he'd say something about me taking forever to get ready anyway, so it didn't matter.

Sometimes he'd say something funny, so I'd laugh and think, *well, maybe I'm making mountains out of molehills.* Regardless of the situation, there was a pattern of him not taking responsibility or apologizing to me. I just couldn't see it clearly at the moment. Things were progressing in our relationship, and I was afraid of messing things up by fighting about things that didn't seem significant at the time.

Using your *frog in the pot* analogy, when did the water start getting a little

hotter?

Brad wanted to move to a new city. He claimed that it would save us both some money. He also noted that he wanted to move *with me,* which felt romantic at the time. I had found a lower-paying job, and the hours varied every day, and it was stressful.

I remember asking Brad if I could hang up some of my pictures in our new place, and he got mad at me. He said that he had already hung up his photographs and that my pictures didn't fit in with the décor now. He threw it back in my face that I had initially told him just to hang up what he wanted. Why was I changing my mind and asking to hang up stuff now?

I tried to explain myself and said that I hadn't felt like hanging anything up at the time with the stress I was under. I remember saying that I thought it was *our house,* and there was nothing of mine decorating our home. I remember feeling hurt, confused, and too exhausted to fight, so I went to bed with tears streaming down my cheeks as I fell asleep.

I remember feeling so beaten down and not understanding why. The front of my forehead would start buzzing and throbbing after disagreements like this, and I would feel anxious and sad. Then he would be nice for a while, and I'd forget we had even fought. Amnesia would set in once again—and the heat in the pot would rise a few more degrees.

Every once in a while, during an argument, Brad would say that he thought I had anxiety problems—probably stemming from my childhood. I didn't know if that was the truth, but I didn't argue with him. He made it seem like I started fights a lot, but our disagreements felt one-sided, and I was left on the losing end the majority of the time. Later on, I would begin writing these situations down to remember them and keep track of how often this would happen.

From one of our earlier conversations pre-interview, you had said that you and Brad had gotten married *in secret* a little less than a year after you had moved. Would you mind telling me more about that?

Brad proposed to me that Christmas and said we should get married right away because he could add my daughter and me to his insurance. This would save us a lot of money in the long run, as my daughter was experiencing some health issues at the time, and her medical bills were kind of expensive under my work insurance.

We had a small ceremony at a county park near where I had grown up. Two of my friends stood as witnesses, and one of his friends was ordained to do the ceremony for us. I remember thinking that it was perfect and was excited to tell everyone. However, after the ceremony, on our way home, Brad told me not to tell anyone.

Why couldn't you tell anyone?

Brad said that his mom would be disappointed that she wasn't invited and that we couldn't tell her yet. I told my family and friends but had to keep it off social media, so no one from Brad's family would know.

How did that make you feel?

I felt confused and upset. I didn't understand why he couldn't just be open and honest with his mom or family. It made me wonder what else he was keeping from them—or me. This also made me feel dishonest, because now I would be a part of a lie telling his family. That breached my honesty boundary, and I felt uncomfortable with that.

Was he hiding anything else?

YES! The following month after we got married, I found out that Brad hid financial debt from me. It was ironic that he had been so overly concerned about my debts before moving in together. The bomb exploded, and I felt angry, tricked, lied to, betrayed. He had been struggling financially for quite some time and said he had hidden it because he was ashamed. I was furious. My mind reeled.

Before we had moved in together, I had to sell my place. He had spent money on flooring for my condo so that we could sell it faster. I'm not sure how much money he spent. I remember telling him I was grateful, but he didn't need to spend much money. He had insisted on redoing the flooring because a few changes would help the resale value.

The year before, he had taken me on a $600 shopping spree. He picked out things that he liked and thought looked good on me. I remember feeling uncomfortable at the time and asked if he'd be okay financially. I had even said that I'd put some things back on the racks. He reassured me that everything was fine and that he could afford it. He even said that I deserved to be spoiled, so it was okay.

I knew that Brad made decent money at his job, but was well aware that he wasn't loaded. I wasn't looking for a millionaire. I was looking to spend my life with someone honest. He had chosen to be dishonest instead.

What? One month after you were married, he dropped this bomb on you? What happened after he disclosed the financial issues?

I lost respect for him and didn't know what to do. He told me on my birthday, when we had friends coming to stay, so he had made the *big reveal* in a moment where I was rendered powerless to have a discussion about it, or figure out how bad it was. I was flabbergasted. I felt like I didn't know him at all.

I now realized that the reason he hadn't moved to the city too far in advance of my daughter and me moving in with him was that he couldn't afford to. He needed a *roommate* to pay the rent. He couldn't afford to live independently with all of the debt he had accumulated but hadn't told me about.

Did Brad ever apologize or do anything to make amends for the financial predicament he had created?

Brad offered no solutions for his financial infidelity. He blamed me. If I had a better-paying job, we wouldn't be in this mess. Had he not had to help me *fix* my condo, he wouldn't be broke. Had I not wanted a *sugar daddy* to take care of me and buy me $600 worth of clothes, he wouldn't be struggling financially. The blame-shifting was surreal. I found myself arguing with him about all of his faulty reasoning and we started shouting at each other. It was clear that he was not going to take any responsibility for this situation at all. In his mind, I should fix this because he genuinely believed that I had created this problem.

Why didn't you leave him at that point?

Because loving couples forgive each other, right? Being newly married and not wanting our marriage to fail, I tried harder. I came up with a plan to fix things. It would take time—years, but it could be improved.

So *YOU* had to fix the financial problem that HE had created?

Yes. He left it up to me to figure it out. Thankfully, one of my strengths is looking at a problem and breaking down the steps to figure out how to solve it. Working quickly under stress is another area where I tend to shine!

Also, as all of this drama was unfolding, my previous employer reached out to me to see if I'd work from home! They were impressed with the work I had done before I had left for the city. They hired me back and doubled my income! I was so grateful for the opportunity to work for my old company again and hopeful about navigating our way out of this financial mess!

WOW! That is crazy and amazing! Did things improve with Brad at that point?

Sadly, no. A month after that, I found out about *more* debt that Brad held. It was a student loan he had neglected to tell me about. His reasoning? "It's in deferment, so I'm not paying on it right now. If I'm not paying on it, why does it matter?" I began to realize that honesty was something we viewed very differently. To him, withholding information wasn't lying. To me, withholding information *was* a form of lying. This, again, turned into a fight. He'd ask me why I couldn't just let this go? Because it had again breached one of my values— honesty.

What happened after you got the new job?

I worked longer hours initially, but working from home offered me the flexibility to do more for my daughter. I felt better about things; I felt happier and had a little more pep in my step! That first year, I made almost as much money as Brad! I thought Brad would be pleased and see how much more I contributed, but it seemed like my success was irritating him instead.

Brad's demeanor changed. He would talk me up and compliment me around other people, but he would trivialize and diminish my accomplishments behind closed doors. He would find fault with housework not being done, or get mad about random things. Instead of him helping out more, it seemed like he expected me to do more because I worked from home. He told me never to leave dishes in the sink and would become very angry if he saw any.

When he would leave his dishes in the sink, I'd bring it to his attention, and he would laugh about it or blame it on the dog. When I got upset about this double standard, he would then turn it around on me. Sometimes he would sarcastically and disrespectfully say, "Okay, Nancy" or "Okay, Debbie" when he disagreed with me.

Nancy was my deceased Mother's name, and Debbie was a co-worker he couldn't stand. When I'd ask him why he was calling me names, I would either be met with extreme swings of silence or anger. Many times, he'd walk out of the room and ignore me.

I never felt good enough for Brad. When I worked from home and wore yoga pants, he'd sarcastically say, "Yoga pants again?" If I had gray hair showing, he'd ask me when I planned on getting it colored. He'd see a zit on my face and make fun of me. He'd call it "Jerry" and ask me how "Jerry was doing." He expected perfection.

When did you realize that what you were experiencing was abusive?

I began to realize that we didn't have a real relationship. It was an *arrangement* with an illusion of being in a relationship. Genuine relationships require vulnerability, love, honesty, trust, kindness, and understanding. What I was experiencing wasn't any of those things.

He never physically hit me, so I didn't realize that I was experiencing psychological abuse (emotional & verbal). I just felt beaten down, unsupported, tired, depressed, anxious, and felt like I wasn't allowed to have feelings or experience my own emotions.

I noticed that he'd never take responsibility for any of his behavior and wouldn't apologize for saying mean things, calling me names, belittling me, or yelling at me. If I was disappointed with anything and tried to talk about it with him, it inevitably would turn into a fight. It always seemed to be my fault. He'd say things like, I was too complicated, anxious, had mental problems, or was bitchy. I started to feel hopeless and stuck.

I only saw my friends a few times a year and didn't keep in touch. I wasn't sure what I was feeling—but I felt like things weren't right. I felt like I was constantly anxious and didn't know what was causing it or fixing it. I thought there was something wrong with me because Brad seemed to think so.

What was the turning point in your relationship where you thought that you might leave him?

There were many things, but two pivotal moments stand out: after being elected to serve on the city council, and an incident on Brad's birthday.

I made a run to represent my district on our city council and won. I looked forward to helping our community and becoming a good leader. I had always wanted to serve in my community on a larger scale and was grateful for the opportunity. However, I felt like I couldn't be a good leader when my husband kept pushing me down emotionally. One time he told me, "You only pursue all of these interests because you need to fill an empty hole inside of yourself." It's like he didn't know who I was at all. I felt like I didn't even know him.

The confusing part is that he seemed to understand other people just fine! I'd hear him have compassion and genuinely care about others—but when it came to me, he could be so cruel. He was the doting husband in front of other people and would hold my hand and speak highly of me. Sometimes, hearing him say these things was shocking, because he'd never tell me these things at home, behind closed doors. It was like we were in a different dimension. The thought of leaving him began to creep into my mind slowly.

The turning point was his birthday. I had promised to take him to dinner earlier in the week. When that day arrived, we fought all day, and he hadn't spoken to me for eight hours. Not wanting to ruin his birthday, I broke the silence and followed through on my promise for dinner. He drove to the restaurant and was chatty, acting like things were normal—as if we hadn't just NOT SPOKEN for eight hours.

After dinner, I was getting ready to pay and realized I had forgotten my phone. I asked him to please give me the tip amount, and I'd pay for the bill. He then proceeded to talk down to me and "teach" me a way to figure out the tip "quickly" in my head. I gave him a blank stare and again asked him to provide me with the tip amount.

His face turned from happy into a red volcano in mere seconds. He then yelled at me and said, "You ungrateful bitch! I am not going to be disrespected like this!" He then abruptly got up and stormed out of the restaurant, and sat in the car. I was in complete shock and felt humiliated. People at other tables stared at me. I tried not to cry.

The waitress looked concerned for me and asked if I was okay. I told her I was alright and that I'd like to pay the bill. I added that she should share the cake with the other staff and hoped they'd enjoy it. (I had ordered it on my way to the bathroom, in secret, as a surprise for Brad's birthday.) I walked out of the restaurant in humiliation and got into the car. The ride home was awkward and quiet. When we got home, I crawled into bed and silently cried myself to sleep.

WOW! Did that happen ever again?

Yes, he started yelling at me more often after that. At this point, the "frog in the pot" was beginning to be boiled. My brain was buzzing pretty much every day, and I felt like my head was going to explode. I felt like I was on the verge of a nervous breakdown. Brad had started a pattern of "rage screaming" in my face over the smallest of things.

I began to feel mentally exhausted. One time, he stopped me from leaving the house and asked me where I was going. I told him I was leaving to put gas in my car. In what seemed like a nice gesture at the time, he said he'd do it for me. I was shocked and happy! I told him that I appreciated him offering to do it for me. However, two days later. He never followed through.

When I confronted him, he turned it around on me and didn't take any responsibility for it whatsoever. It was absolute madness. He screamed with rage in my face when I calmly asked him why he hadn't put gas in my car. I had made the mistake of making a frustrated "puff" of exhaling air and had given him a look of disappointment. This small action had instantly set off a geyser of anger from Brad. "YOU DIDN'T REMIND ME!!!" he raged. I could feel his spittle on my face, and I looked away.

At the end of our relationship, Brad put me down every day; nothing was good enough, dinner was terrible, I was awful, I was raising my daughter wrong, and I was accused of "coddling" her.

His behavior toward me would toggle between I'm the worst person he's ever met, to being thankful I was in his life. It was so confusing and painful. I didn't know if he loved me or hated me. It became complicated to navigate and hard to discern when anything I did would be viewed favorably or unfavorably. Every day I was walking a tightrope, afraid of losing my balance and falling without a safety net. I had no idea what was happening to me or how to stop it.

Still not ready to give up on our relationship, Brad and I attended couples' counseling. Our first session was a failure. It was a Zoom conference. Anytime I would open my mouth to talk, Brad would interrupt me and talk over me like I wasn't there. I asked him to stop interrupting me, and it continued. I looked into the camera and directly at the therapist and shrugged my shoulders.

It was ridiculous. When I was finally allowed to speak, I calmly explained that Brad's behavior was an issue. The whole time I was talking, he looked red-faced like a cartoon character about to have steam blowing out of his ears. He kept constantly repeating that I was disrespectful. That I, being myself, was rude to Brad.

I couldn't breathe, talk, or look at him without being accused of disrespect. I couldn't even tell you what I could have done, or how to act, for Brad to find anything about me acceptable. I found myself pre-thinking anything and everything I did. Knowing that if I made a miscalculation in my speech or action, he'd explode.

It didn't even seem to matter anymore. He had said several times that I was directly responsible for his moods. To this day, I am not exactly sure how I was responsible for his moods. I was always taught that you could not control another person's behavior, but you have complete control of your own.

He would also say things to me like, "You've changed. You aren't the same person I dated in the beginning." I told him that he had changed too. Everyone changes! I don't know a single soul who is the same person they were in high school or college. People change and grow! In a relationship, the hope is that you grow together, and it was painfully apparent that Brad and I had grown apart.

It sounds like you were running out of options. Did you ever think about leaving him?

All of the time! I sent my daughter away for a couple of weeks so I could decide what to do. I planned to talk to Brad and gauge whether or not he could see how his behavior was an issue. If he absolutely could not see how his behavior was negatively impacting our relationship and our family, I would need to call it quits. If he didn't take any responsibility, I had to realize that no matter how hard I tried or how perfect I was, it would never be enough. I would only be subjecting my daughter and me to worse treatment, and providing my daughter with faulty programming on how a man should treat a woman.

I started using Google as a resource to look up topics like: Am I the problem in my relationship? What is a healthy relationship? Is my relationship toxic? Is my marriage making me sick? Am I depressed? Why is my husband always yelling at me? Am I suffering from anxiety? Through reading various articles on these topics, I found a book called "The Verbally Abusive Relationship" by Patricia Evans. The book would become my lifeline to understanding what I had been experiencing all along and why I was feeling the way I was. I cried while reading it, not because I felt sorry for myself, but because I was relieved to find proof that I wasn't crazy.

At this time, I didn't know my daughter was writing journal entries for school as part of her online learning. The last straw was when I received a phone call 20 minutes before Brad and I had an online counseling session. (He was going to attend from his office, and I was at home.) The phone call was from a social worker from my daughter's school. She said she would be emailing me a journal entry my daughter had made and that she was also contacting my daughter's father.

Oh, my gosh! This was all happening within 20 minutes of your Zoom counseling session with Brad?

Yes! I was mortified! I felt sick to my stomach and felt like I was going to throw up. My life was suddenly under a microscope, and at that moment, I felt like I had failed my daughter. The moment of truth had arrived, and my answer to whether or not I was leaving Brad was now glaringly obvious.

I checked my email while the social worker was still on the phone with me. The entry had been about an incident that had occurred while my niece had been visiting. I recalled that day in my head.

My daughter and my niece had been giggling and laughing on the couch while we were playing a video game with Brad. He had gotten impatient because it was one of their turns, and they were being kids and screwing around and not paying attention.

The amount of anger he had displayed towards them had been extreme, and very disproportionate to how the kids were behaving or what they had been doing. I remember freezing and seeing the girls freeze. I saw a tear stream down my niece's face, and I saw my daughter fighting back her tears. We had sat in silence finishing the game, fearing that if we had abandoned the game, more anger would have been unleashed.

Immediately after the game ended, I took the girls upstairs and consoled them. I remember being so confused with Brad's ever-worsening behavior and realizing then that I was running out of choices. The journal also noted that my daughter was scared for me, and she missed me. Tears streamed down my face as I read what my daughter had written.

The social worker put my daughter's father on a conference call with us, and I was forced to tell them what the journal entry was about. I assured them that Brad didn't physically abuse my daughter or me, but that he was verbally and emotionally abusive (not that verbal and emotional abuse was any better treatment).

Before this moment, I had been looking at apartments, but was now in a predicament where I felt like I needed to commit to moving out and putting down a deposit. The journal entry was the last straw. I felt like I was hurting myself and my daughter by staying. We needed to get out.

What happened at your Zoom conference with Brad? Did you talk about your daughter's journal?

Yes. After I got off the phone conference with the social worker, I had to log into my Zoom counseling session with Brad quickly. I remember just cutting to the chase and telling the counselor and Brad what had just occurred and that I didn't think counseling was helping. Brad kept saying something about his reputation and that my daughter's father was behind the journal entry—blah blah blah.

He never took any responsibility for his behavior. Never once did Brad apologize or act like he felt wrong about how his actions had negatively affected my daughter or me. He acted like my daughter and I were fabricating the intensity of his anger or "embellishing" the seriousness of the situation. He would never see his behavior creating pain for his family, and at that moment, I knew we were done.

The picture started becoming more apparent to me. I began to realize that what I was experiencing was far worse than being physically beaten. Physical abuse produces "proof" that something is wrong and who is doing the hitting. However, in my case, I was mentally beaten down, with no proof to show anyone what was hurting me. My psychological wounds would remain unseen to the outside world as I silently suffered.

What happened after the counseling session?

I called the landlord of a property I had looked at and told him I would be giving him a deposit. The next day, I met him, signed the paperwork, and handed him a check.

What happened when you told Brad you were leaving him?

I barely slept the night before I told him. I kept telling myself that I needed to "rip off the Band-Aid" and get it over with. The next day, I waited till things seemed calm and asked him about all of the times I had tried to address problems in our relationship—that they would never get resolved. How three deal breakers had occurred in our relationship and that our marriage was over.

He looked at me blankly and said in a chilling voice, "You'll never leave me." My blood ran cold. I looked him dead in the eye and said, "Well, I put a deposit on an apartment yesterday, and I move out in a month." He looked stunned, and for once, Brad was speechless. We filed for divorce shortly after. I researched how to get a divorce in my county and felt confident that we didn't need an attorney if he agreed to file jointly. Even if he didn't want to file jointly, I would figure out how to navigate the process myself and get it done.

During this time, I somehow managed to still be a supportive mom to my daughter, maintain a high work performance in my regular job, attend all of my meetings, and stay on top of my city council duties. I felt like I was dying inside, yet no one even knew what I was going through, other than a few friends I had finally opened up to. Even they had difficulty believing me, because they had never seen the side of Brad that I had been describing.

That last month, I felt so terrified. I would discreetly pack my belongings into boxes and hide them in my office or closet so Brad wouldn't see them. Even after I was packed, it didn't look like anything was missing. Everything decorating the walls of our home belonged to Brad. I walked gingerly inside the house, afraid that any wrong move would have thrown him over the edge.

I slept in the guest room and put something heavy in front of the door every night because the door didn't lock. I was quiet as a mouse, and even if he got mad about something. I always made sure to be completely calm. He even tried to make me jealous and incite a reaction from me by leaving his computer tablet out in plain sight for me to see.

There were notifications constantly popping up on it from dating websites. It made me feel angry at first, but instinctively, I knew that if I had opened the apps, read any notifications, or reacted negatively in any way, it would only count against me. So I did nothing. Because I didn't respond to his game, he called me cold. It was clear I was in a no-win situation.

That is SOME story! Wow, it sounds like you went through a lot psychologically. What helped you heal through all of this?

My daughter and I both talked to a counselor to work through our emotions. The book "The Verbally Abusive Relationship" by Patricia Evans also helped me regain my sanity. Had it not been for that book, I don't know that I would have been able to make any sense of my experience or have healed as quickly. It also helped me understand how I had gotten myself into this situation and that it was not JUST all Brad's fault.

It took me forty-four years to realize that my parents weren't the best model for relationships. My parents had learned unhealthy ways of fighting and relating to one another. I had normalized this in my relationships when it had occurred. My programming was faulty. My boundaries also needed work. Because I had allowed Brad to put me down, belittle me, call me names, and yell at me, he continued to do it. We teach people how to treat us. No, I didn't deserve the treatment I received, but if I hadn't ALLOWED that behavior from the beginning, and would have held firmer boundaries, I would never have married Brad.

Learning these things has allowed me to rise like a phoenix from the ashes. Because I have a better understanding of myself, I feel more confident. I also feel like I am a better leader and living a life more aligned with who I am. Now I understand the warning signs of toxic people and do my best not to involve myself with toxic individuals.

I don't even hate Brad! I forgive him and wish things could have been different. Maybe he had some faulty programming, just like I did, that made him believe that this was the correct way to treat his wife. I genuinely hope he can learn and grow from this experience, too, so that he may have a real relationship someday that includes vulnerability, love, honesty, trust, kindness, fairness, and understanding.

My friends told me that I made my divorce look easy. There wasn't anything easy about it at all. I went through some trauma and mainly remained calm through all of it, which I cannot explain. My mind had been stuck in complete fear and confusion, and half the time, I felt as though my brain was in a fog. There were so many unknowns, and I had no idea if my next step would only throw me into more of an abyss.

All I could do was trust myself and take one step at a time. I only knew that if I were to stay in my relationship with Brad, I would lose myself, my dreams, and my dignity. One thing that had been certain to me was that I needed to crawl out of the boiling pot of water before it killed me.

I didn't want this to irreversibly impact my daughter—leaving her with faulty programming that would lead her down the same path. I had made it on my own before meeting Brad and had confidence in myself that I could do it again. I was determined to be the frog that would escape from the pot of boiling water.

Thank you so much for sharing your story with me today. It sounds like, despite the odds, you were able to overcome your fears and make the essential choices and connections to leave an unhealthy relationship. Some people never make that choice and choose to stay, despite their unhappiness. You should be very proud of yourself for being strong enough to leave a toxic relationship.

After the interview was over, I felt relieved. I stretched my arms and my back as I got up from the couch. I thought about another song that helped me through this experience. The song is called "On a Good Day," by OceanLab. It's a hopeful song that reminds me that things are already brighter and that I'm getting to know myself better every day. Music is one tool I often use to lift my spirits and help mentally pull me out of dark places.

Leaving my husband was the most challenging choice I ever had to make in my life. The thought of failing at marriage pained me and had kept me in a mental prison, weighing me down like an anchor. I had toggled between staying in my unhappy marriage, avoiding the judgment of others, or choosing to leave and facing harsh judgment, criticism, gossip, and embarrassment. I had chosen the difficult path because it had seemed the most freeing; in the end, it was.

I chose to do this interview because so many other women are struggling out there in toxic relationships, trying to understand what is happening to them—attempting in vain to change themselves enough to make someone else happy. When you have to hide who you are, you never get to discover or display your unique gifts to this world entirely. It makes me sad to think of how many women feel that they have to shrink themselves to please their partners.

Hopefully, sharing my experience will assist someone else with identifying when they are in a toxic relationship, and help them understand when it might be time to leave. If the abusive partner doesn't see how their words or actions are causing pain to anyone else, it is very unlikely that things will ever change.

I looked over to a large circular mirror hanging on the wall. I walked over to it. There, I gazed into the glass. I saw the same kind green eyes and a soft smile— saw the *interviewer* in its reflection. I smiled, and the interviewer smiled back. She had a smile that was big and bright when she laughed. She was beautiful, with or without makeup. I waved at her, and as she waved back, I knew she did her best to find understanding and dig deeper for answers that were not always easy to figure out.

She was supportive and wanted to see a brighter future for not only herself, but for others. She was a woman who had more strength than she gave herself credit for. This woman desires to serve her community, and possesses the ability to become more than she ever thought possible.

She was seeking the answers to how and why she had felt so alone and unwanted when she had so much to offer—making the difficult choice to set herself free and to rise above the chaos—deciding instead to live her life on her terms, free from constant judgment, pain, and the need for perfection.

As I walked away from the mirror, I knew that I would never again shrink myself to fit into someone else's idea of who I should be. I was no frog, and I refused to be placed in a pot of water again—You won't boil me alive.

* In loving memory of my sister Kara *

Chapter 9:

Generations of Impact

By Abbie Lorene

Lost Pituitary Intuitive

Gripping each side, she tugged at her stomach, stretching and pulling it like Play-Doh from side to side. Looking in that long deceptive mirror, I heard, "Ugh, Mom! Do I look fat?" I studied her slender figure, freckled nose, and the way she wore her vulnerability. My eyes started from the middle, working their way up towards her face. I was shocked when the reflection was not of my daughter's waves of ocean-blue eyes but my honey-colored eyes. Both sets of eyes shared a mutually masked appearance of exceptional strengths that neither daughter had yet seen in herself.

At that moment, my thoughts took me straight back to my childhood. Echoing in my head, "Do I look fat in this?" My eyes meet an all too familiar pool of honey. Except these identical sets belonged to different women I loved. I wondered *how often* I had heard my beautiful mother, Michelle, and sisters also say those words? How many times *had* I said those very same words to my daughter? It was déjà vu, in the third generation.

They left me wondering why I could see the beauty in each of them while they struggled to see it, Suddenly, it hit me. As a daughter, and now as a mother, I'm passing on the same generational negative self-talk. It seems, as I grew into my body, it came equipped with two lenses. These lenses acted like a filter of what I was funneling into my brain. One lens has a unique distortion of my image. "This is how you are supposed to look, what size you are supposed to be." However, the new lens was showing me, "These are society's unrealistic expectations for women." I've found myself at times rotating through the day which set of lenses I was putting on.

As I embrace and honor each of my daughters, they will inevitably experience school differently than I did—painful flashbacks bombard and burden my heart. Middle school started my journey of unhealthy peer comparison. Those deep roots began occupying space in my impressionable mind. My body wasn't developing as quickly as my best friends Amber, Missy, and Jenny. My peers always said I was *lucky* I had not hit puberty yet. The first book I remember reading, *Are you there, God? It's Me, Margaret.* I lived in Margaret's hell from the fifth grade to the first day of my ninth-grade year. I didn't want to be a late bloomer; I wanted to wear a real bra!

Every August was like Christmas! It was the rare occasion my sisters and I would get to go on a shopping spree! Grandma Ella would give us a $100 limit to purchase whatever my mom said we needed. Fumbling through the cart at the Kmart checkout, I cringed as Grandma set my pile of clothes on the counter. Quickly, with panic, I shoved a women's navy blue water bra towards the cashier. A water bra was to *enhance* women who were flat-chested, like me. Grandma immediately spotted the bra. "Abbie Lorene, I don't think this was the kind of bra your mother would have approved!" "Nah, it's all good," I said. "Ky has one, Grandma." It was a sad day when that water bra met the dryer.

Each day I would go to school, a barrage of comments about my body flew my way. I swear it felt like nearly every guy in that place felt they had a duty to let me know about my late- blooming body. I now wonder if that was the case, or was I hyper-aware of it because that was my entire focus at the time?

"Yo! Roses are red, violets are blue; why is your chest as flat as your back?" The whole room erupted in laughter. Flushing red face, tears barely staying in the corner of my eyes when the bell saved me. Ringgggggggg! Fumbling through the crowd, I rushed straight to orchestra class.

With my eyes scanning the room, panic set in. I turned my attention towards Mr. Klett, when I heard Amber and Miranda giggling as they waltzed in just after the tardy bell. They, too, had experienced the relentless insults, but my closest friends seemed to melt away all my insecurities. On weekends, they included me in their plans.

Although I couldn't put my finger on it at the time, I had envied each one of my closest friends. They all, at times, seemed ungrateful for what their parents afforded them. I wondered if they knew how privileged they were.

It wasn't just about the paid all-night skate rink trips, stylish clothes, beepers, or the fast food we were treated to. In all honesty, it was more the way each carried herself with a confidence I had only dreamed of. As one of their best friends, I loved them and their families, for they could provide more than just the essentials: power, clean clothes, food, an endless supply of toilet paper, and *two* loving parents.

In the concrete hallways of Teutopolis High School, other kids' laughter would bounce off the walls. I would pseudo-listen to their gossip, complaints of a teacher accused of being touchy, road trips, ring day planning, and boyfriends. Any group discussion of bloated stomachs, stretch marks, over- or under-eating, discussion of weight gain or weight loss, breast size, or body size made me uncomfortable. I would look into the mirror as an outsider in my own body, and I would obsessively stare at my stomach in the mirror, wondering when my peers might find out what I was hiding.

In retrospect, I now see the comments we made as girls and the negative self-talk with a new perspective as a mother and a woman. As a mother, I think about how I have unintentionally degraded myself without thinking my daughters are listening.

When I heard my gorgeous daughter ask me if she *was fat*, it brought guilt to my aching heart. I mean, after so much internal work and external work, I felt like I was winning the war against my low self-esteem, and I was proud of myself. Now, as I heard my own daughter's self-degrading words bounce against the mirror's reflection, it felt like a stab to my heart and immediately transported me back to that locker room.

Every day of that year, I worried, *what if they found out?* There was this big secret I had been hiding. What would they think, and how would they judge me if they knew? I already felt stupid and miserable enough.

I loathed physical education because I had to undress in front of my friends. I would manically chat with the other girls to distract them from looking anywhere but my face. I would slyly slip my shorts on and swap out my shirt bent over, sucking in my tummy. I turned away from the other girls.

Honestly, I thought I was in the clear. I assumed I hid it well. What I didn't know was that my reflection, in what seemed to be 99 mirrors hanging all over, was caught by a classmate. I felt the cold floor underneath my feet and all eyes looking in my direction as my classmate blurted out, "Whoa! What the heck happened to your stomach?" Her eyes were staring at my belly, watching, waiting for my response to her cutting words.

It was finally the moment. The moment I had spent so much time daydreaming about in study hall, of what I would say, and how my peers would respond. I thought up a thousand different scenarios, with only one response from them: Judgment. I know now that it was my feelings of worthlessness and self-judgment I was projecting onto them.

With an uncomfortable laugh, I responded, "I call them tiger stripes. The product of weight gain from giving birth. Consider yourselves lucky that you haven't earned yours yet." Everyone froze in the locker room. I expected all their faces to turn into looks of judgment.

Finally, the classmate said, "What do you mean, Abbie?" I plunged on, without actually answering the question. "Before anyone assumes anything about me, just know I did what I know most of you are doing. I just happen to be the one who hit the jackpot with that 1% not guaranteed when using protection. It could easily happen to any of you at any moment. Having sex even once creates this."

As my last word fell from my lips, they understood I was saying I had given birth. Many of their eyes dropped to the floor and away from me.

After I answered their invasive questions, I was proud of myself—proud that I was able to stop hiding the adoption of my first son. I loved my son beyond measure, to the moon and back. He was never meant to be a dirty secret. I wanted to be truthful with the whole world, keeping his memories alive with me and those who had loved him with me. The essence of that was so vital. As each birthday, holiday, and Mother's Day passed, it was a very dark and stressful time while I learned to navigate life as a birthmother.

During this time, the anxiety, loss, confusion, and depression lead to suicidal thoughts. I learned so much about myself during this season of hell in my life that made me want to FIGHT for my future. Giving life by giving away my son for the best life he could have is a devastating level of grief. It wouldn't be until six years later, when I had my daughter, that I would understand how much I forfeited my right to be a mother to my son.

As I held him in my arms, I got to feel what it was like to do it right. I am not saying what was suitable for me is right for everyone. Choosing adoption was right for me. Some teen moms have the proper family support and are more prepared to be a mom than I was. I have a friend whose teen daughter has chosen to keep her child and is an amazing mother.

It took almost ten years of counseling, countless tears, stressful, pressured choices for my future, before I would fully heal and believe in my heart that I had done the most selfless act of love in my life. It was the most difficult decision of my life. I knew I was bettering myself (and him) and that my decision was the right one.

While I was dealing with my grief, I did not always handle those feelings well. Self-harm and sabotage were my *poor* coping skills of choice. I was quick to snap at people or be critical of those around me that I loved. It was like being swallowed whole, and anxiety pulsated in my mind, heart, and chest.

I was drowning in a cesspool of negativity and comparison, and I would choose to shut out the world. There are so many things to be distracted by in those moments when negativity creeps in. I think to myself, *I can't be the only one that gets sick and tired of hearing their phone buzz and go off.*

All these distractions and coping skills lead to burnout. The burnouts were happening more frequently, so I decided I needed some help. I chose to get counseling. I decided to be honest by digging up those negative roots holding me in a stagnant position. When I dug up those roots, my mind seemed to release a tidal wave of sadness, anger, grief, and heartache. Memories came flooding back from what others said to me. Eventually, my mind began the process of releasing horrible words I used to say to myself.

These negative words were like a weight trying to pull me to the bottom of the ocean. They were drowning me in feelings of worthlessness. I had to release the weight and swim up to the surface, to find a lifeboat with others who could pull me in.

Through counseling and support, I gained a set of skills that I've continued to add tools to ever since. I utilize these healthier tools, though not perfectly. I have gone back to old ways of thinking sometimes. I struggle to compare myself to others and am left feeling less than them. And this comparison and self-loathing was what I was passing to the next generation.

I no longer want to sit around and lie to myself: *If I just lost five more pounds. If I wore this shirt that didn't make my belly look so flabby, then I could love myself!* My biggest insecurity, the flab underneath my arm; when I wear tanks and see a picture of myself, all I see is the extra skin spilling out of the seams. And the sagging of my breast from losing weight.

My life partner asked me just to see me the way he saw me. He shares how amazing I am. How I help those in need—even if it comes before my needs. He sees me as a forgiving person—a woman who is a super mom—someone who has incredible talents and strengths. When he says these things, the generational echoes of *you don't deserve those compliments* would try to dismiss them. I still battle those thoughts, but with work, they have become fewer and farther between.

Even now, as an adult, I feel like I am supposed to have it all figured out. However, I can still be a bit of a mess. As a partner and mom, I'm needed consistently by many people for various reasons, and I don't always remember to take care of myself. It's almost as if I seek out those in need while putting my needs off to the wayside.

I realized I needed to value, love, and make myself meaningful. But, how was I going to become more self-aware? I will let you in on my best-kept secret: Instead of spewing out ninth-grade harmful or destructive thoughts and allowing myself to hear them, think about them, or believe them, I write them all out of my mind and into a document on my computer. There are days my hands can't type fast enough and seem to vomit on the screen. Once they are out, I can see how wrong they are. I can begin to refute them one by one.

I also know I need to fill myself with love. When I find inspirational quotes, pictures that lift me, music that heals and makes me think, "Yes, girl!" I add that positive beauty to the document. More and more positivity is there because I am looking for it. Whatever you are searching for, you will find.

With a hostile critic and imposter syndrome, you will find just that. Get it out of your system in healthy ways, and you'll see that the vastness can be filled with light and positivity. I've accepted my flaws, set a vision into motion, and am now betting on my strengths.

Now that you know your worth, choose your circle of friends to show how each will play a critical role in lifting and supporting you. You do not need to lean into all this healing alone.

I could not be more thankful for the women who have directly or indirectly inspired my ever-changing perspectives during this journey. I knew I needed to ask certain women to help keep me accountable, to find that joy and happiness in life. Truthfully, that took drinking a shitload of humble Kool-Aid on my side, to seek out and ask women for help, but it was worth it. I am worth it!

My beautiful long-lost sister Kallee. My grandmother Ella, and my mothers, Michelle, Robin, and Sandra. Tasha, Vanessa, Amber, Melissa, Rachael, Tori, Kristi, Alicia, Alyscia, Hannah, Khloe, Nicole, April, Abreanna, Aspynn, and Destyni were those beautiful women that helped keep me accountable to find positivity, joy, and happiness in my life.

Iconic boat-and-float days on the lake with Carly and Molly were the most therapeutic self-care days. My soul soaked in the magnitude of Nature's beauty while unplugging from the world. These women are my biggest cheerleaders, pushing me closer to my goals each day. Missy was so proud of me for pushing through as I navigated the ups and downs life brought my way. I will forever be grateful for her encouragement to write and share my story. The pain of missing her is a beautiful reminder of the joy of loving her.

For me, knowing that there was someone to help me was foundational. Remember that it can be anyone from your family of origin, or the friends who have become your family, who will love you unconditionally as you move forward, supporting and encouraging you through it all! Each woman will unknowingly play a different, yet crucial role in elevating you into places you dreamed of. Done correctly, she'll be inspired and elevated simultaneously.

I've now set myself up for success. I am choosing joy each day, self-care, therapy, support groups, and healthy coping skills. But I don't want you to think life always follows the plans we have for it. One of my daily visual reminders is an awareness art I have had tattooed on my arm. It reminds me of how capable I was, even when I didn't think I was. When others see it and ask, I share my story. It creates a space for them to share their stories of strength. We are entirely connected as warriors.

Putting in internal work, going to therapy, and being fully honest and transparent about my struggles has me sitting entirely in a vulnerable red zone. Finding myself in an abyss of chaos made me realize I needed to protect my peace. I call it *Putting feet to faith*. There are times in the healing path that all I can do is put one foot in front of the other in full faith, as complete darkness surrounds me. But I get up, and I choose to do it anyway. Each day, I set my feet onto my hardwood floors; I start oozing joy. I am blessed. I am grateful to have another day with all the people I love, adore, and admire.

At times, life takes unexpected turns. We find ourselves in situations we could have never imagined. Our lives have surprising moments—good and bad. When these things happen, please reach for someone higher than yourself—lean on a Higher Power, reach fiercely to stay anchored, and utilize and build your network of supporters who will be there for you.

Remember, tomorrow is never promised. Stop waiting for the perfect time to accept, embrace, and love your whole self. When the pessimistic words crept into my mind, I pushed through them. Constant wonder swirled around, feeding my insecurities of whether I was loved or accepted. It was a never-ending record that never seemed to stop.

My pain & struggles of self-love have now become my purpose.

Have you ever told yourself:

- *If I just lose a couple of pounds,* or

- *if I could just look like her and tone up into better shape,* or

- *if I could be "this size" or weight under,* or *if I did XYZ,*

- *Then, I would be worthy of love, and comfortable in my skin.*

I can tell you from experience, saying that in your head, it will continuously cycle through and make you think you're *not good enough,* until you won't do what you're created to do. For me, it took forever! It took me thirty-five years to finally tell myself that I wasn't going to wait to get skinnier, healthier, less wrinkled, or less grey to live my life unapologetically. I wasn't going to miss out on the fun. I wasn't going to wait to take pictures. I was going to look in the mirror and love what I saw.

I don't want you holding back from doing "that something!" That thing could be anything. Maybe you want to create a bucket list or a vision board for your dreams and aspirations! If you haven't yet made something like this, *Stop!* Look around! Grab a writing utensil and a piece of paper and write down ten things you want to do!

1.   6.

2.   7.

3.   8.

4.   9.

5.   10.

You can't skip this—do it! I'm waiting. Are you done? GREAT! I am so proud of you. Now, put a star next to the top three of the things on your list that seem impossible. Now, write down the barriers you will overcome to allow you to do these three things.

Imagine how your life will change when you accomplish these three things. Imagine how your actions will change those around you. When we do the internal work for ourselves, we change our story. And that then gives our daughters the ability to choose their stories. Sis, let's break the generational body -shaming cycle together.

As I embodied my journey, I remembered all the good and bad things about high school. What made the most profound impact was all the negative words that bounced off the concrete walls. Through my daughter, I know this is still happening. Imagine if, on those concrete walls, you could visibly see those words. Words have power!

While I was thinking about this one day, an inspired mission came to me in a flash of feelings. If hurtful words have power, so do loving, compassionate, uplifting words. What if the wall of every school were covered with positive, personal expressions from others?

I want to start a movement in these schools and call it, "You're worthy, and you belong!" My movement would:

1. Create peer building, meaning we would teach our teens how to build self-worth in each other. This helps to build up the future women they will become.

2. Build self-worth, which could be done anonymously and directly by complimenting something special they see in that girl in some unexpected way.

3. Display the positive compliment or positive affirmation in a variety of ways in the school: on the wall, as bathroom posts, on doors, above classrooms, along with scrolling information displays, newsletter emails, texts, and or even on PA announcements at the beginning of the day.

4. Post the information by keeping it viewable every day for each beautiful, unique girl to see that their value in themselves is a critical part of the movement.

Instead of teenagers basing their worth on what they can do (grades, teacher approval, or going to the online social media platforms—the negative cesspool), my movement would teach them their intrinsic value.

Our worth was determined before we ever came to this earth. Girls, teens, and yes, women, listen up! You are loved because you have a life! Your life is worthy of love, no matter what you do—your self-worth and value are *not* based on your actions. You are worthy of love because you have life—you are light! These youths are valued.

My program would encourage peers to send out those comments, compliments, likes, and positive affirmations daily, and in a way that each person gets that positive love every day. Knowing you have worth is so powerful, and I can't wait to bring this movement to your youth as soon as possible.

If I could go back to that moment when my daughter was looking in the mirror, judging herself as "not good enough," there is one message I would want her to have. It's the message I want all of our daughters to have. I would look at her in her deep blue eyes and say, "I want you to be loved by yourself. I want you to realize that no person can love you better than yourself! Tomorrow is NOT promised. STOP waiting for the perfect time to accept, embrace, and love your body and self."

If you would like more information about this fantastic mission, please reach out to me at miss.author.abbie@gmail.com

Dear reader, thank you for coming along on this part of my healing journey. Writing for this book is one of the things on my bucket list I never thought I would do. I'm so proud of myself. (See what I did there?) I am so proud of you! I would love for you to share with me how you unconditionally loved yourself today. You have the power to inspire the women you love in your life!

I have a few wise words once shared with me that led me to finish this book. "Set down the fear and lead forward with courage."—Al Church, my high school & college English professor.

You are unconditionally loved, and worth it!

Chapter 10:
Self-Care for Caregivers
By Cindy Strom
Anxious Gonadal Counselor

It was a busy day on the unit: multiple admissions, very few empty beds, a fast pace. I finally got a chance in the shift to grab a coffee and check my phone. I checked for messages more regularly since things with Mom had become more complicated. There was a message from Dad, and my mind raced. I knew he was home alone with Mom, and things had been getting worse. What I didn't realize was that the trajectory of our lives was about to change drastically.

As I held the phone to my ear, I heard my dad's voice. He sounded stressed, almost panicked. Mom was confused, he breathlessly explained. She left the house wearing only a light shirt and pants, no shoes, saying that she needed to get home to her parents. Her parents (my grandparents) passed away years ago. Dad urgently tried to guide her back to the warmth of their home. It was January in Wisconsin and happened to be a brisk, negative one-degree temperature that day.

Mom had become increasingly confused over the weeks and months before this, misplacing things, forgetting details and entire events, perceiving things, such as people stealing from them or breaking into their home. But, up to this point, she had consistently recognized my dad, my brother, and me.

On this day, she didn't acknowledge Dad and thought he was a stranger trying to harm her. She became combative and resisted him. Somehow Dad was able to get Mom back into the house, but she still didn't recognize him as her loving husband, who was trying to help, not harm her. She was frantic, throwing things and screaming at him. He needed help.

I called, and Dad picked up the phone right away. He still sounded breathless. Mom had become passive for the moment, seemingly unaware of what had happened barely an hour before. I told him I would be there as soon as I could. In the meantime, we made a plan that Dad would call 911 if things escalated again.

I still had five-and-a-half hours left in my twelve-hour shift at the hospital. Like all my fellow nurses on the unit, I had an assignment of patients that I was responsible for. I explained the situation to my charge nurse, who listened empathetically as I discussed what was going on. She could have been doing a thousand other things at the moment, but took the time to listen and help me collect my thoughts. Fortunately, a few patients would be discharged, and assignments could be switched around to accommodate my leaving early.

An hour later, I was on the way to my parent's home. It was a 30-minute drive to get there, and I barely remember the drive itself. I was anxious about what I might walk into as I stepped through the door. Would Mom be disoriented and upset again? Would she be calm? I needed to have a level head in this. What was the best course of action? All of these things went through my head as I drove.

I arrived to find Mom standing in the living room, calm but out of sorts. She didn't recall what had taken place between her and Dad. It was gut-wrenching to see my mom like this. She was herself, but she wasn't. At that moment, she could not piece together in her mind where she was or what had happened, but she still recognized me.

She seemed disturbed as she silently tried to grasp what was going on. I gently explained to her that we needed to get help. As I tried to explain what happened that afternoon, she remained confused but understood that Dad and I were concerned. Thankfully, she agreed to let me drive us all to the emergency room.

In the ER, Mom received a thorough assessment, blood tests, and a head CT scan. She was admitted to the hospital for the night, pending more tests in the morning. None of us knew how long her hospital stay would be or what would come of it. I had thoughts of what was going on for a long time, but up to this point, Mom didn't have a diagnosis.

I phoned my brother later that night. He is also a healthcare professional who works at a hospital in Mississippi. We had been seeing him more frequently than the usual 2-3 times per year, as he traveled to Wisconsin to help with Mom more often these days. Exhaustion was setting in as I relayed the events of the day. My brother planned to be back in Wisconsin within the week.

The next day started early. Mom was seen by the geriatric resident, geriatric fellow, and the attending neurologist and gerontologist. Many tests and studies were ordered. Mom was pleasant, even welcoming, when the doctors rounded. She politely answered their questions. Sometimes her answers made perfect sense; other times, it was as if she pulled together random thoughts and was trying to put them into a reply that would suffice. No matter what the conversation was about or who the specialist was, Mom always had the same questions for them. "Why am I here?" and "When can I go home?" It was painful to see my once strong, resilient, fun-loving mom in this place, not knowing exactly where she was, why she was there, and why she couldn't leave.

Dad and I did our best to be at Mom's bedside during her hospital admission. As the days wore on, Mom became restless and increasingly confused. Her replies in conversations often didn't make sense. The doctors referred to it as confabulation, a symptom of memory disorders in which fabricated memories fill in memory gaps. Mom told some wild and colorful stories that, to her, made perfect sense. Many stories involved memories from her childhood that Mom thought were in the present time. She frequently mentioned having to get home to her parents. Some times were particularly devastating, when Mom would have moments of clarity and would tearfully confide that she thought she was "losing her precious memories." Other times she would ask, "Am I going insane?" She was distressed and scared. One night, after arriving home, I called the unit for an update on Mom. The nurse told me that Mom was "pleasantly confused." Let me tell you that nothing was pleasant about this.

During this time, I was working full time and visiting Mom when I was off work. Dad was going back and forth to the hospital every day. When we weren't at Mom's bedside, she would wander out of her tiny hospital room and into other patient's rooms. Sometimes she would be agitated and rant about things that she perceived were going on.

Mom thought everyone was out to get her. She didn't trust the hospital staff and didn't feel that she needed to take direction from them. She often would talk of shootings happening outside, or the police having to be called for a disturbance. None of which took place. The nurses did what they could to keep Mom calm, but the truth is, they couldn't simply attend to one patient for any length of time. They were responsible for many patients at a time. This situation was not sustainable, but Mom wouldn't be discharged until we had a diagnosis and a treatment plan.

It took almost a week to get said diagnosis. I arrived at the hospital after work to find Dad in the hallway outside Mom's room. She was sleeping, and he took the opportunity to stretch his legs. He was tired. Over those last weeks, I had watched as the dark circles under his eyes grew, how he stood a little less straight, how his breathing had become a little heavier, and how fatigue seemed to wash over him. In a steady voice, Dad told me that we finally had a diagnosis for Mom. She had Alzheimer's disease.

Having a diagnosis gave us something to work with, at least, but one doesn't just get discharged after that. A "safe plan," as the doctors referred to it, needed to be in place before Mom could go. She wasn't able to care for herself, and she was a safety risk, as well as a flight risk.

This gave us two options for a *safety plan*. One was to turn my parents' home into a memory care-like facility, with locks on the inside of doors leading outside, putting locks on the stove, and absolutely nothing in the house that she could harm herself with. This also meant piecing together round-the-clock daily care. As I watched my dad's health decline by the day as a caregiver, I knew this would not be our option.

The other option was to place Mom in a memory care facility. The thought of that conjured up so many emotions. Grief for the loss of my mother as I knew her. Fear for what lay ahead for Mom. Fear that I (we) would make the wrong decision on her behalf. I felt helpless that I couldn't fix what was happening to her. It felt like all we could do at the moment was react.

It was challenging to process the feelings I had during this time. My days were consumed with work, visiting Mom, and trying to quickly educate myself on what to look for in a memory care facility. Grieving the loss of my sharp-minded, funny, caring mom would have to wait.

How was it that we had arrived at a time and place in life where we were charged with deciding to have Mom live in a "facility?" I didn't want to be responsible for this. Who was I to be part of making this decision? It felt so awful and wrong. I felt guilty for even considering "placing" Mom somewhere other than her home. As my dad, brother, and I tried to get our heads around this, another problem presented itself.

For someone to make medical decisions for another person, including where that person should live, there must be a durable medical power of attorney in place. My parents had always planned well. They each had a will, a living will, a durable power of attorney, and even a health care power of attorney. But something was missing: a designated health care agent, someone specified under the health care POA who could make decisions for an individual who has become incapacitated, or unable to understand or make decisions for themselves. This was not something my parents had.

Even if that document had existed, it would have needed to specify that the person deciding on Mom's behalf could admit her to a nursing home or long -term residential facility. So, even though Dad and Mom were married, we would need to go to court to get Dad appointed as a guardian and obtain a protective placement order.

At this point, we were over a week into Mom's hospitalization and needed to get moving on a plan. Dad would handle the financial end of things and contact an attorney to help with the court proceedings. I was in charge of dealing with the medical side of things and finding a place for Mom to live.

The first person I turned to for help was the hospital social worker. I needed information about memory care facilities and how one transitions to this new environment. The social worker was warm and friendly but spread very thin in her role. As I sat in the hospital conference room hoping for information about what I should do next, the help I received came in the form of a pile of papers placed in my lap with the brief explanation, "These should help."

I was overwhelmed. As a healthcare professional, I felt like navigating all of this would be easier. Sure, I understood medical language, disease processes, and how the healthcare system worked, but working with Alzheimer's and dementia patients was not my specialty. I had limited experience in assisted living from nursing school clinicals, but I had never even been in a memory care facility. How was I ever going to find the best place for Mom?

Later, at home, I sorted through the papers I received. There was a pamphlet from a company that helped in finding a community for your loved one. I reached out to an advisor at the company and was given a list of facilities within a specified area. They also offered to make appointments to visit facilities. Having someone who had a list and could make appointments was helpful, but it all felt somewhat transactional, instead of personalized and caring, as the brochure had described.

By the following day, I was provided with a handful of communities for Dad and me to start touring. We had little idea what to expect. I had a shortlist of questions prepared that I figured would refine as we toured different places.

Dad and I turned into the parking lot at the first community on our list. It was midafternoon on that cloudy, cold day. I was determined to be focused and present, despite my swirling emotions. I had done a pretty good job keeping it together emotionally up to this point. It served me well to compartmentalize my feelings, to show up as solid and competent. But on this day, the grief and sorrow were right on the surface. I felt raw. This whole thing was just so surreal.

As we approached the front door, the first thing Dad and I noticed was that it was impossible just to walk in. Visitors, actually everyone, needed to be let into the locked facility. We rang the bell. The administrator greeted us and introduced himself.

We stepped into a small entryway, then into a common living area that had no one in it. It was dreary, with very little daylight flowing in, and had shabby furnishings. I came to this place with realistic expectations. I wasn't looking for a five-star resort, but I wanted a place that would feel comfortable and homey for Mom—and me. I needed it to be a nice place—a place where we could take mom and feel confident that she would be cared for with dignity and compassion.

As the administrator led us through the facility, I noticed that most residents were in their rooms. How much time did they spend out in the living area? What kinds of activities were scheduled? There were also things that I was not prepared for—like the sounds and smells. I could hear residents talking, some quietly mumbling to themselves. The lunch hour had passed before we arrived, leaving a scent that reminded me of a hot lunch in my high school cafeteria.

As we continued, we would get an occasional whiff of soiled adult diapers. In other areas, it was evident that bleach solution was the cleaning agent of choice. As someone who works in a hospital, none of this was shocking, but I was experiencing it in a different context. This wasn't where I worked; this was a place that I was checking out for Mom to live. It was hard being there with that intention. I wasn't comfortable like I was in my work environment where I'm the one helping. I'm the well-versed one. I help people make a plan. At this time and place, I needed help, and that feeling of vulnerability was uncomfortable.

Dad and I were able to have a discussion with the administrator after our tour. He had likely heard stories like ours many times, but he listened with empathy and concern as we relayed the course of events that led us here. He was able to address our questions and concerns. At the end of the conversation, he provided a list detailing what it would cost to have Mom live there. Pricing varied depending on what level of care an individual needed. Mom was still ambulatory and could do some self-care, so she would require less assistance from staff than someone who needs full assistance with positioning, bathing, and toileting. We knew memory care would be expensive, and that was confirmed. The cost would be around $4,000-5,000 per month to start. Prices increased with increasing care needs.

The best way to describe how we felt after leaving was numb. It was a lot to take in. We needed to take a break and think about what all of this meant for Mom, and us.

After updating our list of questions, I checked into a couple of other places that didn't even seem to be at the standard of the first place. I felt like I was hitting a wall. I needed to hear a familiar voice—someone familiar with my family and health care. I phoned a dear friend, whom I have known for many years. I absolutely should have reached out to her sooner, but things were moving fast, and it simply hadn't occurred to me until now.

My friend is an RN who works with elderly individuals and is very familiar with assisted living, nursing home care, and memory care. She provided the clarity and advice that I needed, with a healthy dose of caring and compassion. She also looked up a couple of places on the list of facilities I had been given.

It turned out that those places had been previously cited with the state of Wisconsin for safety violations. That was good to know. Last, but not least, she named two areas that had consistently good reputations over many years. I was beyond grateful for her kindness and generosity. With that, I was able to proceed with a new sense of hope that maybe this could work out, and we would find a place that was a good fit for my mom.

The following day, Dad and I toured one of the places my friend recommended. We were cautiously optimistic. We were greeted by a warm, cheerful administrator, who explained that she had been caring for individuals with memory issues since she was much younger, as she had helped her mother care for multiple family members with dementia while she was growing up. She guided us to her office for a chat before touring the facility. Her level of empathy was palpable, and her expression showed that she truly knew how it felt to be going through this with a loved one.

This time the tour felt different. It was still challenging, picturing Mom anywhere else than at home with Dad, but I could see that this place felt more like home. Light streamed in through large windows and patio doors. The common areas were thoughtfully decorated and had a cozy feel. Framed pictures of residents and staff enjoying activities hung on the walls.

There were large oval tables for residents and visitors to dine at together, and the smells from the kitchen were fantastic. The living room had plenty of comfortable furniture, a piano, and lots of room for activities. An activity calendar was posted on the wall that showed an impressive schedule of daily games, crafts, chair yoga, entertainment, and holiday celebrations.

The administrator explained that the staff prioritizes having everyone out of their rooms as much as possible and encourages participation, if able and willing. There was also a fenced yard with a large patio, gardens, and mature shade trees that would get plenty of use once spring and summer arrived.

When we left that community, we felt different. Dad and I knew we didn't need to look any further. If Mom was going to live somewhere other than her home, this was everything we could ask for.

The following week, Dad and I were scheduled to appear in court for the guardianship and protective placement hearing. Dad had hired an attorney who was experienced in this type of matter. She was also able to expertly guide Dad through how to properly split up marital assets to pay for one spouse in memory care without the other spouse becoming impoverished in the process. We needed legal help with all of this, but the level of knowledge, professionalism, and care our attorney displayed was top-notch. We had everything we needed for the hearing and would go into court feeling confident that the judge would approve the guardianship and see the need for protective placement.

On the day of the hearing, our attorney, Dad, and I entered the courtroom together and took our seats in the front of the courtroom. Once again, the whole thing felt very surreal. I knew this was something we had to do, but it felt like we were going behind Mom's back. It also felt final, as protective placement meant that there would be a court order, authorized by two physicians, to have Mom in memory care.

Never in my life did I think I would be part of such a thing. I just kept telling myself it was to get Mom to a place where she was safe and cared for, where I knew my dad's health wasn't declining in the process.

During the proceeding, our attorney did most of the talking. Dad and I had to confirm a few facts and details, but it all went very smoothly. The judge was personable and compassionate. In the end, I understood that having a dad as Mom's legal guardian and protective placement order in place was the right thing in this situation.

At last, we had our plan in place, and Mom could be discharged from the hospital. It took two more days to tie up loose ends at the hospital and gather personal items to take to Mom's new community. During this time, we were worried about how Mom would react to all of this. It still felt wrong to have made all these arrangements without her being a part of the conversation. She couldn't have understood what was all taking place by that point, but it still felt awful, and if my mother were in her right mind, she would have hated every bit of this new plan.

The day Mom left the hospital marked three weeks that she had been an inpatient on the geriatrics unit. It was a relief to go. My brother was back in town and helped Dad move Mom and her things into her new room in her new community. It was an emotional day for all of them. Even though we were grateful to have found this wonderful community, hanging pictures on the wall and putting clothes in the closet of a room that now belonged to Mom was sad.

Mom didn't understand what was happening. She knew this wasn't her home but couldn't remember where her last residence was. At one point, she thought this was a new house that she and Dad were moving into. She cycled through a range of emotions. She would be pleasant and curious at once, and then she would become tearful and even suspicious and accusatory of her family conspiring against her. The confusion and uncertainty were too much for Mom to handle, especially when there were times that she was aware of her disorder.

We were advised that it could take weeks, even months, for people to become "settled in." In the meantime, there could be restlessness, confusion, anger, and grief for Mom. There certainly was plenty of suffering to go around. It was tragic to go through this, knowing that Mom wasn't simply unaware of what was going on anymore but was suffering and scared as her mental health declined.

For about a year, Mom had ups and downs emotionally, as she became used to her new surroundings. She enjoyed being involved in all the activities and even had her unique jobs, like folding laundry and helping the staff clean up the dining room after meals. However, there were times when she would march out of her room with bags packed and demand to *go home*. There were also times when she would walk out the front door, setting off loud alarms throughout the facility, and stubbornly refuse to go back in.

It's been over four years that Mom has been living in memory care, and during that time, she has become steadily more confused. She requires more assistance and direction with personal care and activities. She isn't as sure-footed as she once was and needs a steadying assist with walking. She is settled and recognizes this place as her home.

The dust had settled on the acute, urgent situation. We found a place for Mom to live, and she had "settled in." In the midst of this, my partner and I moved to a new home. My dad sold the condominium that he and Mom lived in for many years, and he moved to a rental property within minutes of where my partner and I now live.

As the drama in our lives seemed to subside for the moment, I had more time to reflect on the events that had taken place and found myself in a funk. I didn't have anything urgent that needed to be done and felt a lack of direction. "Coming down" from it all was brutal in its way.

During the most intense moments with Mom, we just had to act and get things done. Suffering on your own time was almost our motto. There wasn't much time to go deep into grief, and it wouldn't have served us well to do that at the moment. Now that there was time to process it all, I struggled. I didn't want to keep reliving those difficult experiences, but I needed to process all the lingering emotions.

I also had time now to go deep into brain health and learn more about neurodegenerative diseases. As the daughter of someone with Alzheimer's, I wondered what that meant for me. I figured I'd up my game in the longevity department. I started reading books and listening to podcasts on the subject and was amazed to learn how much control I could have over my quality of life as I aged.

I also explored personal development and read books from Tony

Robbins, Brendan Burchard, and others. This might sound cliché, to go through a traumatic event and then go down a personal development route, but it's what I needed, and it helped me process the lingering grief and emotions.

Through all of this, I started evaluating my priorities in life. I was craving a change. I knew that I could change my health and longevity trajectory and be less at risk for developing a neurodegenerative disease by changing my lifestyle. I also realized that I wanted to help others who were going through challenging situations like mine. I started exploring ways to do this as a side hustle, or even as a new career.

Not everyone thought this change was a great idea. I had a good, stable job in a well-respected field. I had a purpose in my chosen career and worked in a leading community hospital. Why would I want to change that or give that up? I get it. This wasn't something I was taking lightly. But, some significant things had taken place that revealed a new path that I was growing increasingly passionate about.

The need for a change had been coming for a long time. I knew there was something else for me. I knew I needed and wanted something different. I loved being a nurse and caring for patients, but I was growing tired of the state of healthcare. Staffing shortages, unsafe work environment, hospital administration seemingly unconcerned about any of it made me weary.

During the weeks to follow, I searched for other ways to help and serve others. I became a Certified High-performance Coach, trained by Brendan Burchard and a personal development coach. This was an avenue to entertain my passion for helping people, eventually becoming more than a side hustle. I loved working with new clients and could see what a powerful program I had become trained in. Clients were getting transformative results in many areas of their lives.

Still, I felt there was something bigger that would come of all of this. Then, one early morning, as I woke up, I had an idea. It's as if this idea was just waiting there for me to wake up. It was clear as a bell, with details that formed into a vision of what was to come. I would build the business I needed when my family and I went through the grief and anguish of placing Mom in memory care.

It would be a business that would help and support families who had loved ones with Alzheimer's or dementia. I would walk side by side with people struggling to navigate this journey in an empathetic, personalized way. I sat up in bed and grabbed my journal and a pen from the bedside table. I began writing as the ideas about this business flowed over several pages. I made lists of services, people who I could reach out to, and diagrams.

Ultimately, this vision shaped a service-based business that assesses each unique situation to make a personalized plan. Help with strategies for care, tactical assistance such as making phone calls and appointments, preparation for community visits, suggestions of care facilities that are vetted for safety, and emotional support are provided.

Client needs such as lawn service, household care, maintenance, meal delivery services, and support groups are addressed. The goal is to get a plan in place to allow caregivers to keep their own lives up and running, and also be able to show up as the son, daughter, or spouse without having to take on all the rest of the tasks.

Getting this vision on paper was exciting. I felt inspired and hopeful for the future. But there was a looming question: How does a nurse become an entrepreneur? How do I bring this idea to life? I didn't have a business background, but I knew how to find information.

I started researching how to create a small business. I also started networking and talking to people about their experiences as caregivers. Networking in groups and one-on-one opened up a whole new world for me. I met so many amazing people who were supportive and encouraging.

Many people wanted to help in some way, or connect me with others who could help or collaborate. So many others were kind enough to share their personal stories with me—all of this breathed life into my idea. I was able to connect with an attorney who helped me set up an LLC. I found mentors, a business coach, and many new like-minded friends passionate about helping one another succeed.

I received some much-needed straight talk from my mentors, as well. Being an entrepreneur is hard, they all said. It's up to you to create everything that you want your business to be. It's up to you to figure out when to ask for help. It's up to you to be the problem solver, find the clients, market, and sell. Some told me it would take longer than I thought to build my business.

A friend described being an entrepreneur as living by your hand or dying by your hand, which made me nervous. This all was scary as hell. But this idea continued to stick with me, and I made consistent steps toward making it a reality.

Over the last two years, I've continued to work as a nurse, and during my time off, I have worked on developing myself into the person I need to be to run a successful business serving others. As I've been building my business, I've struggled with intermittent imposter syndrome and limiting beliefs. They have almost gotten the best of me on occasion. But I've never thought of quitting as an option. When I get overwhelmed or stuck, I have people I can reach out to who will talk me off the ledge, so to say. I am eternally grateful for these people.

My clients are caregivers who want to do everything possible for their loved ones and keep up with their obligations. I help caregivers who feel like they don't know what to do or where to turn—who are afraid they will make the wrong decisions for their loved ones—I help them overcome that. I support them by teaching them self-care is their priority as they continue to meet the demands and obligations of caregiving and their own lives.

Do you know someone like this? Is this yourself? It is okay to admit it. This is one of the first steps in self-care, to own that acceptance. Please share this chapter with those you know, and here is my email: cindy.strom@gmail.com. Let's get you on the pathway to self-care so that you can care. It will help more than you know.

Looking back, I realize many things. When my family was in the thick of things with Mom, I was not prioritizing self-care. I didn't think I had time. I am so grateful to have had (and still have) a fantastic partner, who took care of things at home and did his best to take care of me, because I wasn't eating, sleeping, exercising, or relaxing well.

Through personal development work and plenty of reflection, I've learned that I wasn't doing anyone any favors by not taking care of myself. Even if I could have made a few simple shifts (like incorporating breathing exercises, stretching and movement, and healthier food choices), I would have managed my stress more effectively, processed my emotions better, and showed up better for others.

Asking for help isn't a sign of weakness. It's a sign of someone who is aware enough to know their bandwidth and recognizes when they have too much on their plate. It's a sign of strength and humility to understand that you can't do it all and do all things well. The "I-can-do-it-myself" attitude is just your ego getting the best of you.

I know now that showing up for myself is showing up for others. Asking for help is self-care. It's okay to let people help you. It fills their cup when they can help, just like caring for others fills mine.

These days, when I'm in a stressful situation, or when I'm feeling overwhelmed by certain events, situations, or simply have too much on my plate, there are specific questions that I ask myself. I reflect on what I tie my worth to, which, in part, is taking care of others. Then I ask myself, *Have I been showing up as my best self for others? Have I also been showing for me?*

From there, I can prioritize what needs to be done, and when.

You can do this, too. When faced with a situation that challenges you, ask yourself what you tie your worth to. If it's all about taking care of others, realize that you need to care for yourself to be your best for others.

What are some things that you could take off your plate that you're not passionate about?

What gives you energy?

What drains your energy?

My last word of advice: Don't wait until you're hitting a wall and too burned out to reach out for help.

Chapter 11

Big Wheel Business

By Laura Hulleman

Lonely Adrenal Interpreter

Do you remember your first bike? To me, riding bikes has always felt like freedom. The tiny bit of danger, speed, silence, and air rushing over my skin as I propel myself forward with minimal effort always makes me think, "This must be what flying feels like."

My first bike was a Big Wheel. Big Wheels were low to the ground plastic tricycles that were super popular in the 70s and 80s. Every part of them - the frame, the handlebars, the back two small wheels, and the signature front Big Wheel - was all poured from a plastic mold. The pedals came right out of the middle of the Big Wheel, and the only speed limit was how strong my little 5-year-old legs could pump it. Fortunately, my bike was not the Barbie-colored pink and white version, but the "Superman" red, blue, and yellow version.

I remember getting on the Big Wheel tentatively at first. My cousin, who was three years older, could already ride a two-wheeler and do so much faster than I could. She would start riding down the block, yelling, "Come on!" and I would pedal a little faster each time. There was only one way to stop a Big Wheel. You locked your legs, stopping the pedals, and allowed that front wheel to drag across the pavement until you stopped.

The first time I locked that front wheel to stop, it scared me how the little trike slid on the pavement. But I didn't tip, I didn't get hurt, and it was also kind of exciting. The ride down the block, I went even faster. It became fun to see how far those plastic wheels would scrape before they came to a stop. My hands hung on stronger, my legs spun faster, and my squeals of delight were deafening.

On that Big Wheel, I developed my signature superpower. The 180 DRIFT! I was the only one of my friends that could slide that back end around in a 180-degree total U-turn. If you shifted your weight while stopping, the back tires, which were also plastic, would slide to the side. I can still hear the sound the plastic tires made as they slid across the pavement, and I spun wildly.

The first time it happened was an accident. I shifted in my seat as I was stopping, and it drifted a little to the right. I was scared, but I didn't tip, didn't get hurt, and I was also so cool! I was driving as Bo & Luke Duke did in my favorite 80s TV show. Don't judge me for my love of the Duke's. What did you watch in the '80s? "A-Team?" "I Dream of Genie?" It was not a great time in entertainment.

Whole afternoons were spent practicing that drift over and over, crushing any fear. I went up and down that block, building up enough speed, locking the front tire, and confidently sliding the back end around. There is one problem with learning to ride any bike, even a Big Wheel. You are going to fall off. Do you remember your first big crash on a bike? I remember it like yesterday.

I came to the end of the block, and I pushed a little too much with my hips. The rest feels like it happened in slow motion. The Big Wheel started tipping past the point of return. As it flipped, my knee made contact first with the pavement. I felt searing pain as I left little pieces of my skin on the pavement instead of plastic wheels. I flew off the tricycle, with my sunbaked little legs flying over my head. When I came to a stop, my cousin was speeding toward me on her bike. My little 5-year-old body crumbled on the ground, crying. Adults were called from the house, and my mom scooped me up into her chest and held me close. "What happened?" she lovingly asked.

"I wiped out!" I howled.

"You are going to be okay," she reassured me. Do you remember skinning your knee as a child and knowing you were going to die? Looking at my legs, I saw missing skin and blood. She saw dirty hands and a skinned knee.

She carried me inside and washed my wounds. "Just a little scratch," she soothed. Could she not see the very obvious *skin peels*? It was cleaned, dried, kissed, and bandaged at my insistence. Then my mom said the most bizarre thing I had ever heard. "All better, you can go back outside and ride your bike again."

WHAT?!? Had she not seen what just happened? A bike was indeed the most dangerous toy known to Man, or at least a child. It didn't even have a seat belt, for goodness sake. I was NOT going to ride that bike ever again! And I didn't ride that bike again—for at least an hour.

We played on the swings instead. But then my cousin got back on her bike and rode away. The fun of riding was calling me back, and soon that call became more powerful than the fear of falling off.

I LOVED that Big Wheel, right up until the day I rode the front tire right off it. I was so sad when the adults proclaimed the giant holes in the front tire made it unsafe to ride. Remember, there was no rubber lining on that front tire. So, every time I stopped fast or spun around, I wore a bit more of that plastic off—sometimes things have to end.

Waiting for the Knowledge Bomb

Fast forward forty years to a small conference room and a women's networking group I was attending. The speaker that day was Teresa Romain, a coach that I had worked with before. In her talk, she was comparing money and abundance to a tricycle. That is what I wanted in my business: money and abundance. One small back wheel was the logic; the other was your intuition, alignment, and flow. However, the big front wheel was where all the movement happened.

As soon as she said, "big wheel," I was immediately transported back to the freedom, fun, challenge, danger, and excitement of my Big Wheel. Where was all that in my business? I had the logic and systems; I had the intuition, alignment, and flow. But I didn't have any freedom, fun, and excitement. My business was in a state of being stuck.

I am the creator of the Endotype Formula on which this book is based (more information in the introduction). Sitting there listening to Teresa, I had three years invested in research and development. This new personality profiling system was finally done. I knew coaches were my primary clientele, and I knew this system could transform the work of coaches. I had no doubt the formulas worked for people.

What I didn't know seemed to outweigh what I did. I didn't know how to explain what the Endotype Formula was. I didn't know how to market this massive concept to coaches. These formulas were so rich and deep; I didn't know which part the coaches would buy. I knew this information was essential and powerful, but I didn't know how to expand the company to support it. How could I do all this?

So, I listened closely to my friend and former coach as she talked about money and abundance being like a tricycle. This is what I wanted for my business. I was barely breathing as she spoke. I didn't want to miss THE knowledge bomb, that one thing that would click into place and make my business work.

Have you ever found yourself sitting and waiting for that one more thing? The right moment, the right coach, the right speaker to "fix" whatever is broken? I know now that it is not very often one truth bomb will click everything into place. Usually, it is more like learning how to ride a bike up and down the sidewalk. You end up doing the same thing over and over and over until, finally, a light bulb turns on. Enlightenment happens in small increments of movement, not one click of knowledge.

As Teresa wrapped up her talk, I was still waiting for the two-by-four of truth to set me straight. You could say I was disappointed, but it was something more than that. I could feel energy and emotion rising in my body. I felt myself trying to control the frustration, expectation, contempt, and anger I felt vibrating through me. What was wrong with my business? What was wrong with me? Had I just invested all this time into something that wasn't even going to work? It wouldn't be the first time.

Many people approached Teresa afterward to talk to her. I watched for a moment; she was by herself, so maybe she could give me some clarity. As I started speaking, I didn't even know what I wanted to ask. I told her I loved her talk, trying to make my voice as happy as I could. I noticed my words speeding up as the story of my Big Wheel spilled out of me.

She kindly looked at me, a little puzzled, and said, "Actually, Laura, I was talking about a tricycle, not a Big Wheel. But I'm glad you got something from the talk." "No!" I thought, "She doesn't get it." I could feel a moment of confession approaching.

My eyes started to burn as I explained. I felt like I had everything she said we needed. Small tire of logic, check. Small tire of intuition, check. Big tire getting it moving, check. I had been working for three years to make this work, and somehow it wasn't. My throat began to close, and the tears that formed in my eyes spilled out and down my cheeks. "It's not working ... I have everything in place ... all the parts, just like you said, and it's not working. I don't know what to do. What should I do? What am I missing?" I watched her face soften as I squeaked out my confession. She had placed a reassuring hand on my shoulder, with an "I've been there" look.

The Endotype Formula was done, ready to be used, willing to do good work in the world, but was I ready? Ready to try again? The tears that ran down my face were from my fear and knowing that I was holding back. This fantastic research could help so many people, and I was holding it back. A wave of possibility followed the fear as I managed to choke out, "Maybe it's time for us to work together again."

The End Of Things

This was not the first business I had ever had. My whole life, I have been serially self-employed. I experienced a measure of success with each business. And I found a lot of things that didn't work for me. I tried reupholstering furniture, being a mortgage broker, I was a freelance makeup artist, and network marketer. My advice for everyone is: Don't hold yourself back by "What will people think?" Jump in, try new things, and learn about yourself.

One of my businesses ended with me injured, sobbing on the sidewalk. It was also the one with the most potential, the most success, and the most fun. It all started after the birth of my second child.

I had put off going back to work as long as I could. I didn't want to be away from my kids all day. Our bank account said it was time for me to go back to work part-time, but I didn't want to get a *nights and weekends* job. If I did, I wouldn't see my husband ever again. I wanted something with flexible hours, above-average pay, and maybe I could bring my kids along if I needed to.

It took me a couple of weeks to realize that was precisely what my personal trainer had. After I had my son, I hired her to lose the "baby weight" that I carried my whole life. All of my training sessions were scheduled around her schedule. Sometimes, if she didn't have a sitter, she brought her mini trainer (daughter) to the gym. And I knew what I was paying her. It fit all my criteria. But I didn't know if I could be a trainer. Up until hiring her, I hadn't ever gone to the gym. So I did the only logical thing, I asked lots and lots of friends their opinion, hoping they would talk me out of it. This is what I now call giving away my power. Do you give away your power? Where in life do you look for others to make your choices for you, perhaps disguised in asking their opinion? The great benefit of this is when something doesn't work out, you can blame it on the other person.

But this time, no matter how many obscure people I asked, everyone thought I would be a great trainer. Eighteen months later, I was not only a trainer but owned a women's training studio. I opened it in 500 square feet of my big downtown home. It was a great location, and best of all, there were no extra overhead costs to running my gym there. It consisted of two rooms and a small half-bath. In the big room, which was not that big, I packed my fitness equipment and would train 2-3 women at a time. I would do consultations in the small room, and while I trained, my kids would play or watch cartoons.

I trained lots of moms who loved that they could bring their kids with them. I helped these women gain strength, both physical and emotional. They began to prioritize themselves through our work, knowing they were just as important as their husbands or kids. They lost some weight along the way, but this became secondary to the confidence I would see in their eyes.

One hectic morning, the little 12ft x 25ft space was packed. I had two women warming up on the cardio equipment, three in the middle of the workout, and two stretching out. I couldn't move from the corner I had been exiled to and was directing the workouts from there. One of the moms said, "I would like to get out and start running with my daughter, but I don't have a jogging stroller yet."

"Oh, I have one! I don't use it anymore because my boys are too big for it. You can have it. I'll bring it here and leave it for you the next time I work out." That is when I realized I hadn't built a gym; I built a community of powerful women supporting each other. What an amazing thing!

I had started to follow a lot of fitness experts. To create a profitable business, all the experts said you need a bigger space and some employees. After being open less than a year in my 500 square foot studio, I expanded. I brought on two employees and moved to a 2000 square foot space. When the women I trained had begun asking if I would ever do anything for men, I knew better than to turn down income. So, I divided the space and started a kickboxing studio that men could attend, also. I was so good at following all the advice.

Running a much bigger space took up more of my time. Clients started wanting early and night classes, which I provided them with. The customer is always right! My kids spent lots of time at the gym, I saw my husband a little less, and my take-home profit dropped. But I was building a business! The experts kept saying it takes three-to-five years to build profitable businesses.

I didn't worry, because it was working after all. The space and training times started to fill. It was challenging to find the right help and keep them, which meant filling in many of the classes myself. However, I told myself that every owner makes sacrifices and just look at the good I was doing. Clients began to ask when I would expand or open another location. "Everyone needs to experience this." That idea was so intoxicating. Had I finally found my business superpower?

With a lot of encouragement and a giant financial leap, I signed a lease for a prominent 3600 square foot gym space. This move almost tripled my overhead, but I was confident. Every time I expanded, the people came. I changed my business model in this new location. I moved away from a boutique training studio and began to offer low-price classes and gym memberships. It required more staffing and more clients, but I was building something.

Managing staff turns out to not be a superpower of mine. I thought everyone who shared my vision would also share my work ethic, but they didn't. It was more stressful trying to cover the expanded overhead. I was working way more than part-time hours now. The gym was pretty much where my kids lived, and they didn't like that.

Have you ever been so absorbed in a project and suddenly realized everything had gone wrong? While I was busy helping others at the gym, something terrible was happening at home. My husband was slowly growing more and more unhappy with being a family man. I had been working so hard I didn't even realize the Big Wheel was flipping.

During one of our many arguments, he said, "When I get done working at the end of the day, I don't want to have to take care of the kids."

I threw my hands in the air and said, "They are your kids!!! We made them together. We agreed I would work evenings. Who else is going to care for them?"

"I want more alone time," he demanded. I soon found out what he wanted was to be single again.

As he pulled further away, I became emotionally and physically exhausted. My home was not a haven for me; in fact, it became unsafe. My business was not a haven for me; it wasn't even fun anymore. Three to four days a week, I got up at 4:30 am to train clients and ended my training day at 6:30 pm. It felt like my life was scraping off layers of skin on both sides of my body— my husband from the right, and my business from the left. I knew I had to start caring for myself, which would mean some very challenging decisions. I divorced my husband, became a solo mom of two kids under 10, and closed my gym business within months of each other. It was tough ending my marriage and saying goodbye to my clients that I loved dearly, but it was such a relief when the skid finally came to a stop.

If I am telling the truth, I knew for a long time I had decisions to make. I told myself I was postponing the choices to give me time to make them. It simply prolonged the pain. Take a look at your life. Where are you delaying a decision, thinking if you wait, get more information, or try one more thing, maybe it will all work out. What is the cost of that delay? For me, it was an energetic and emotional *skin peel.* I left significant parts of myself scraped across the sidewalk in that marriage and business.

It left me with a certain amount of bitterness. I had been working so hard, doing everything the business experts said to do, trying to be a great mom and wife, and it still didn't work. I was angry and looking for someone to blame. Who is your go-to blame catcher? The economy? Your spouse? Your education? Your parents? God? Who do you shake your fists at in frustration before you are willing to take ownership of your own choices? How long will you stay angry and bitter? For me, it was about a year.

Healing My Scrapes

As grown-ups, when we crash, our mom rarely runs out and scoops us up into her chest, washes our wounds, and kisses us. We feel it is a badge of honor to pick ourselves up, wash ourselves off, slap on a Band-Aid, and keep going. I was fortunate to have a support team of friends, coaches, and family that I had kept close to me. Each, in their way, picked up a piece for me. They told me to rest, or took the kids for a while, or helped me do laundry, or mow the lawn. Without that support, I am not sure I would have been able to fully heal from this business (and personal) wipeout.

Do you have a support system, or do you tough it out yourself? We tend to glorify isolating ourselves when we need support by calling it "being tough" or "putting on your big girl pants." Where is the glory in loneliness? If another woman in your life needed support and didn't ask for it, would you believe she is tougher? A better question is, if someone asks you for help, do you think they are weak?

If you have never assembled a support team, how do you do it? You can hire professionals in the form of counselors or coaches. You can join support groups in your community. Another simple way is to call a few of your friends and say, "I am going through a hard time. If I need help or to talk, will you be on my support team?" Notice I said "simple," because it may not feel easy. You can meet in person or through video messaging apps or social media. I have had the privilege to be in a private Facebook group to support a friend diving into some deep trauma.

I sold the big house downtown, which I started my gym and my family in. I moved outside of town to a small but beautiful condo in the woods. My condo is three stories up into the treetops with wall-to-wall windows in the living room and a cozy wood stove. My boys and I are surrounded by state parkland. Every day we discovered something new. Turkeys, hummingbirds, fawns in the woods, woodchucks living under the steps, even the garter snakes became a delightful discovery (as long as they weren't doing that creepy slithering thing near me). Nature's healing energy embraced us everywhere we turned.

I started cleaning homes as a part-time income, and I received money from my divorce. Both combined, I was able to support my family. I was home every morning with my children. And I was home every night with my children. We snuggled on the couch and had movie nights. I was there for their homework and home-cooked dinners every night. And slowly, we started to heal the wounds of the divorce.

I truly believed all the wounds I suffered from were from the divorce. I started slowly realizing how wrong I was. One day, I woke up feeling cranky. It was a rough morning getting the kids off to school. I raised my voice and made more demands of them than usual. I could tell something was percolating right below the surface.

When I got home, I paced the house, trying to find something to do that would stop the rising tide of feelings. I went and stood on my deck. There, with the forest outspread before me, something broke. I was surprised by the first sob that gagged out of my throat.

My tears fell hot and bitter onto my hands as they gripped the rail of the deck. I was finally feeling the whole weight of all my feelings. Closing my gym made me feel like a failure. I thought I had disappointed my clients and let down all the future clients I had yet to help.

My ego was severely bruised. My heart tore like it had a *skin peel*, and only I could see how serious it was. I knew, even while I stood there sobbing, waiting for absolution, these thoughts were wrong. But they were still there.

This gym was not something I did; it had become who I was. The roles I filled there - owner, trainer, coach, inspirer - became how I identified myself. When the gym closed (and my marriage ended), I lost all semblance of who I was. When I made what I did into who I was, what I wanted became unimportant. What I did for my clients, community, and family became how I derived all my significance.

I have not met anyone who doesn't identify themselves with a role they play. Mother, wife, Christian, singer, realtor, American, swimmer, writer, etc. What are the roles that make you who you are? Do you see the danger waiting for you in that? What happens when you lose the job, kids go to school, disagree with the policy, become disabled? You are so much more than the roles you play. You are curious, powerful, intelligent, resourceful, loving, fearful, capable. You are all these, and so much more.

With all my roles stripped away, I was left questioning who I was and what significance my life had. Those questions needed time and healing to answer. As I write this, I am not sure I have responded to them entirely yet. And I am not sure I ever will fully know the answers. What I have learned is that I am significant by simply existing. I also realized I have superpowers to share with the world that have nothing to do with a gym.

Riding Again

It was tough deciding what to do for employment again. Starting another business seemed like a risky and potentially painful process. One morning over coffee, I made a plan; I would get a job. I knew where I would apply, how I would position my offer, what changes I would like to help make in the business. I laid it all out.

Then I thought, "What if one of the boys gets sick?" Their dad had already made it clear he was unavailable if they were sick or had to go to an appointment. In all reality, it was easier to do it myself than to convince him he should.

"Will they fire me if I have to take care of my kids?" I wondered. Then my brain went utterly still. "What if ... they have ... a dress code?" The thought made me shudder, and I realized I was unemployable. Working for someone else wouldn't be fun anymore.

It was as if my serially self-employed self was riding ahead of me as my cousin used to, calling back to me, "C'mon! It will be fun." "Okay," my heart called after her, "but not so fast this time."

I made it my mission to do business differently, more deliberately my way. Right then and there, I realized something important about business. Just like my Big Wheel, the thing that made it go was me! I was both the rider and the engine. If I wanted it to go well in my business, I had to build it as the foundation and make myself the priority.

Even while I still owned my gym, an idea started to emerge. I was fascinated with personality profiling systems, and I had a favorite I like to use. In conversation with a friend, we discussed new ways to type people, and new patterns emerged. Together we played with quiz questions. We tried a quiz with five simple questions on all the clients in my gym. Interesting ways emerged from those results. I learned that 80% of my gym income came from three (out of sixteen) types. At that moment, I knew if I could figure out why, I could sell that to other trainers and coaches.

Now settled into my new life, I was ready to begin developing that idea into a business. It was a slow process. One at a time, the right researcher, speaker, course, or conference showed up where I learned a little more. Over three long and challenging years, the Endotype Formula fully developed. I understand why specific Endotypes are attracted to others. I could see how that applied in the coaching industry. And I learned so much more. I was once again practicing riding up and down that sidewalk.

While researching and building the Endotype Formula, I was also doing all the things I loved. I bought myself a kayak, so I wouldn't have to wait for someone to take me fishing. My boys went on great adventures and vacations. We went to the lake and played on weekday afternoons. I never feared I would get fired if they were sick. After sacrificing so much of myself for so long, I learned how to nurture myself.

Teresa and I did start working together again. One of the first things she did was ask me a seemingly simple question: "What do you want?" I explained to her what this Endotype Formula could do, who it could help, how it could grow. She nodded, but simply said more deliberately, "What do you want?"

I thought I had just told her. So I stopped to think about that answer. A thriving business, healthy family, remodel the kitchen, etc. That is not what Teresa was asking. She wanted to know what I WANTED. I talked about things I wanted for my business, my future clients, and my family. I AM NOT MY BUSINESS. What did I want for ME?

That is when I realized what was holding back the Endotype Formula. I was afraid that I would have to sacrifice ALL of myself again to have a successful, thriving business. I was making it an either-or choice. Either I could have a successful business, or have peace, ease, and joy in life. I was either riding toward one or the other. I had yet to figure out how to have both.

What I wanted then, is what I desire now. I want a business that doesn't rob me of my life. I am finished choosing between my clients and my children. If I want to go kayaking on a weekday afternoon, I will do it. I want clients, my children, and MYSELF to all thrive. I want a business that supports me while I build it. I want to feel supported while I do meaningful work.

What about you? What do you want? Maybe you are like me, thinking the question was, "What are your goals?" You can probably name your goals, but what do you believe you have to give up to have your goals? We make things "either/or" in life instead of AND. What have you given up or sacrificed, thinking the long-term payoff would be worth it? In career and business, we glorify the sacrifice, never questioning if it is necessary.

"Is all that possible?" I wondered aloud to Teresa. "Can I have all that and a business that works?" She assured me that I could. She assured me that abundance meant a life (including business) of ease, joy, and peace. As she described it, I could feel my Big Wheel calling me again. What I desired was a business of uncompromising FUN! I wanted to enjoy the thrill of the ride from my company.

Riding Lessons

The first thing I had to learn was that my business was powered by me. Like riding a Big Wheel, I am the motor that makes this business go, and to do so, I follow my Endotype Formula. In my previous companies, I followed the advice of all the experts; after all, they are the experts. In doing so, I deferred to them, instead of following my design.

The problem with following industry authorities is they are not you. Seems pretty obvious, but even when we know this, we defer to them. Remember, just like people, no two businesses are the same. You will not share the same Endotype Formula as most experts. Your design is unique. Trying to run your business their way is like peddling your Big Wheel with someone else's legs. It just doesn't work. When they say, "Oh, just do this, it will be super easy," what they are saying is, "For my Endotype, this is simple." Because of the difference in design, what is "super easy" for them may be almost impossible for you.

Think of advice like a food buffet with many dishes and vast amounts of food. It all looks and smells lovely, and you are excited to try new things. Still, you don't eat each dish because some you dislike. And you would never think you must eat until the food is gone; you would find yourself sick. There is a veritable buffet of non-stop advice out there. It is not your job to learn and apply it all. Instead, ask yourself, "What here works for me? Does this feel authentic to me and the way I run my business? Does this fit my Endotype Formula?" Use what works for you; ignore the rest.

The next lesson I learned in my new business is that I had a signature move. On my Big Wheel, it was my 180 Drift. My cousin was always faster off the starting line and usually beat me in a race. Her signature move was speed. But she could never do the 180 Drift; she never even tried. In my business, there are things I do very well. My superpowers are speaking, empowering coaches to identify and serve their ideal clients, seeing patterns in behavior, and understanding more significant applications for the Endotype Formula.

There are also things I don't do well. When it comes to editing my writing for spelling or grammar errors, I stink! This fact used to bother me a lot. When others would point out mistakes, I would feel ashamed. The shame stemmed from comparison. Why could others see the errors that I couldn't? I lied to myself, saying, "Perhaps if I just try harder, then I will be able to." I didn't need to work harder. I had to accept that precise details are not my strong natural suit. I could do a lot of things, but that was not one of them. Editing is not my signature move!

I now outsource things in my business (including editing) that are not my signature move. What about you? What are the items in your business (or life) that only you do? I am not talking about things you *should do*, but something you love doing. Identifying your signature move will make life fun and productive.

Once that was identified, I had to practice staying within those limits. I already told you I had a bad habit of comparing and lying to myself, thinking I could do more if I just tried. Setting boundaries for myself and others allows me to prioritize my desires. In my training studio, I put everything others wanted above me. I thought I was less important than my clients, trainers, and spouse. I said yes to things I didn't want to and should not have done. "Could you come in earlier (or stay later)?" Sure! "Can you take the kids with you to the gym tonight? I want to go out after work." Okay!

With no boundaries, I built an unhealthy, codependent relationship with my business which began to suck my life away. I was exhausted and resentful. Resentment and bitterness led to a bumpy and painful end of my training business.

I am determined not to make the same mistakes this time. When I am asked to do something, or participate in events that are not my strength or will benefit me, I say no. Then I practice meaning it. This can be difficult if it is one of my coaches challenging me. Sometimes it is a trusted business associate who offers a "great idea" for my work. I have learned to stop and discern if things are in alignment with me right now. If there is no alignment, I don't do it.

Where do you hold back from saying no? Do you relax your boundaries to "keep the peace" or not disappoint people? Are you still deferring to those you respect who are telling you the right thing to do? To hold boundaries, continue to ask yourself, "Is this part of my signature move?" Boundaries allow you to have a healthy business and life. You will find you also cultivate healthier relationships with people. The result for me has been a better use of my time and growing business.

The last lesson I learned is that just because you leave the skin on the pavement doesn't mean you stop. I cannot imagine all the fun I would have missed out on if I had given up bikes after my first scraped knee. When I closed the gym, I felt like a failure. My soul was injured. But injuries heal, and it's ok for things to end. Notice I didn't go open up another gym. When something ends, it does not mean you have failed. Sometimes it's an upgrade. When my Big Wheel was retired by the adults, I got a blue two-wheeler in its place. I couldn't do the 180 Drift anymore. But when I lock the breaks with that two-wheeler, the hard rubber tires would leave five-foot long marks on the pavement.

What life occurrences are you still calling failures instead of endings? How will you know? There may be pain, resentment, anger, and a tendency to look for the blame, still. What would it take for you to see those situations differently? Please understand that endings may be painful, but you will find lessons and blessings if you look.

C'mon! It Will Be Fun!

After I would get my Big Wheel going, the momentum would pull me forward. Peddling wasn't as hard, and it felt like flying. It was loads of fun! The hidden secret of business is that it is supposed to be fun. There are challenges and effort, but overall, ease. If you are not yelling, "Weeeeeeeee!" inside you after a great day of work, you might be doing it wrong.

What if you don't have a business? Rest assured, you still have a Big Wheel. It may be a career, parenting, partnership, or community involvement. Take a minute to ask yourself, "Am I having fun?" Remember that you power this thing, and you have to do it your way. Learning more about your design is what will make it fun! Do more of whatever brings you delight! Know your limits, verbalize your boundaries, then hold those, even when others test them.

I don't think we can get through this life without leaving a little skin on the pavement. We all tip the Big Wheel from time to time. When it happens, though, know you don't have to pick yourself up alone. Create a support system of friends, family, coaches, therapists, and partners. Let them know when you are hurting. It permits them to call on you when they tip over, too.

My friend, I hope you ride so hard and so fast you wear a hole in your tires. Remember, we are grown-ups now and can just buy another Big Wheel. Happy riding.

Endotype Q & A

What do the words in the Endotype titles mean?

Some have expressed that they don't like their Endotype title, or they feel judged, even. That is not the intention. Each word of your title is important.

The first word in the title, Powerless, Stubborn, Lonely, etc., is your Red Flag word. This describes a feeling you have within that should be a signal for you to stop and get centered. If you begin to experience this Red Flag word, but keep pressing on, you may begin to make choices that don't serve you.

The endocrine gland that most closely runs your body is the second word of your Endotype title. I call them Endotypes because of this endocrine system connection. The endocrine glands and nervous system are the primary ways your brain communicates with your body. Each endocrine gland predictably connects to part of your subconscious mind. This is one part of the Formula of your design. Where you store weight, health problems you may have now or in the future, and your overall shape are determined by your Endotype. If you have a Balanced Endotype, your nervous system is your primary communicator.

The first two descriptors (Red Flag and endocrine gland) are used twice each in the 16 Endotypes. However, the third word in your Endotype title is your unique describer. There is only one Manifestor, Visionary, or Counselor. It also describes what you do well, and at times can do to a fault. You may use this descriptor to "help" others, even when they aren't asking, to gain influence, power, or belonging.

Which Endotypes are most like me?

In this book, we have authors from 10 of the 16 Endotypes. If your type is not represented, or to gain more insight, you may want to read a type similar to you. There are two ways to find similar types:

1) Find an Endotype with a similar title. If the first or second words (Powerless, Stubborn, Lonely; or Balanced, Pancreas, Pineal) are the same, your motivator or inner emotional cravings will be similar.

2) Find an Endotype with a shared orientation. The 16 Endotypes can be divided into four orientations. This orientation determines what your initial thought process is. Know that we all possess each of the four orientations. This just predicts what comes first in your thinking.

Action or Doing Orientation

Powerless Balanced Conductor   Emotional Pancreas Protector

Angry Thymus Visionary   Lonely Pineal Defender

Motivation or Why Orientation

Lost Pancreas Captain   Anxious Balance Builder

Stubborn Pineal Clarifier   Overwhelmed Thymus Harmonizer

Information or Idea Orientation

Powerless Gonadal Oracle   Lonely Adrenal Interpreter

Emotional Pituitary Contributor   Angry Thyroid Manifestor

Feeling or Energy Orientation

Stubborn Adrenal Provider   Overwhelmed Thyroid Enhancer

Lost Pituitary Intuitive   Anxious Gonadal Counselor

Can I have my friends, family, or partner take the quiz?

Of course. We encourage you to share this quiz and book with as many people as you know. Just have them go to www.mywalkmyway.com to take the quiz for free.

Where can I learn more about the Endotype Formula?

If you are interested in learning more about the Endotype Formula, how it works in business, or how it could help you, look us up. You can find us on Facebook, Instagram, YouTube, and at our website www.endotype.com

I am always eager to speak to professionals who want to use the Endotype Formula in their marketing, branding, or to elevate the work they do with people. I look forward to connecting.

Notes

7. *The Star Thrower* (1978, Times Books (Random House) hardcover: ISBN 0-8129-0746-9, 1979 Harvest/HBJ paperback: ISBN 0-15-684909-7, Sagebrush library/school binding: ISBN 1-4176-1867-1); introduction by W. H. Auden

Author Biographies

Beth Kille is an award-winning singer-songwriter from Madison, WI who has been performing her original music since 2000. In addition to performing with the Beth Kille Band, she is also a member of the trio Gin, Chocolate & Bottle Rockets, and the band Kerosene Kites. When not performing, Beth serves as the Music Director for Girls Rock Camp Madison, the co-founder/producer of Flannel Fest, producer/engineer at Studio Gusto, and is a mom. Her mission in life is to inspire all to embrace their creativity.

Mindy Wilson lives in Utah with her three young children, who keep her active life full of laughter. She is a paraeducator at a local elementary school for special needs children. She loves that each day is an opportunity to inspire and help children reach for the stars, while being an example. She obtained her Associate degree from Provo college and is currently working on her Bachelor's degree in Elementary Education and Special Education. When she is not working as a paraeducator, you can find her at the park with her children, working out, crafting a speech for motivational speaking, or writing while blasting empowering music/motivational speakers.

Mindy struggled to find her own distinct voice and passions in life as a young woman and adult. She suffered from low self-esteem and imposter syndrome, trying to find her group where she belonged. She survived a 13-year domestic violence marriage, with every form of abuse. Her voice was temporarily silenced while passions and dreams were locked away. Through this trial, she gained a love for writing, and a deep passion to help other victims of domestic violence and educate the world through advocacy. Her philosophy in life is: "We all have a story within us that can destroy us or help others, so why not use it bravely?" Today a transformed woman, Mindy uses her voice as a survivor and mother to empower people to take their trials and use them for good.

Mindy is a children's author and you can find her book, "Jane Leaps Through Headaches," on Amazon this year. It follows a young girl and her passion through competitive gymnastics in the midst of migraines. Connect at instagram@thedragonflyeffectpage or facebook@thedragonflyeffectpage

Michelle Saunders grew up in Bremerton, Washington with her mom, Diane, and her younger brother, John. She learned to navigate, at the age of seven, a chronic life-threatening auto immune disease, type 1 diabetes. She was previously married to a childhood friend, and while married to him they lived in Pullman, Washington. She returned to Bremerton, where she met her partner in life, Jeremy. After a whirlwind time of dating, she moved across the country to the seacoast of New Hampshire. They have two children, Thaddeus and Magnus, with a six-year age gap. The boys keep them hopping through life.

They are an evangelical Christian family, and are learning to love people for who they are, not what they or society thinks they should be. Michelle is passionate about raising the two boys to be kind and contributing members of society in a positive way. Educating people on the differences between types 1 and 2 diabetes, and helping those who don't have a voice, are two of her big passions in life.

The passion to help others came from her involvement in her church youth group, as well as being a member of the International Order of the Rainbow for Girls as part of the Assembly, Manette #94, in the jurisdiction of Washington and Idaho. She leaves you with this: To love people like Jesus loved the unlovable, and to be of service each day.

Wendy Herrmann has spent most of her career in training and higher education, most recently as a training coordinator, career coach, instructor, and facilitator. She is passionate about helping others learn and grow. Her educational background covers political science and policy, literature, student counseling, and educational leadership. She is an open-minded, life-long learner and enjoys new challenges. Wendy lives with her farmer-husband, Jon, and chocolate Lab, Penny. She enjoys reading, podcasts, Dave Matthews Band, camping, outdoor walks, puzzles, and recently conquered the art of breadmaking (almost). Wendy is diving into the world of writing and

cannot wait to see what comes on this new adventure. You can reach her at:

WritingWithWendy@gmail.com.

This chapter is dedicated to Jon with my whole heart. Special thanks to CB, MJ, and KL

- I will never be able to express my gratitude.

Lisa Nelson grew up in a small town in West-Central Wisconsin. She went to UW-Stout for Graphic Design and has been living in Madison, WI over 20 years. Lisa has a very creative soul and enjoys time with friends and family, traveling, architecture, cooking, live music, and nature.

She was adopted as an infant and had an amazing adoptive family, but has struggled with unresolved medical issues for most of her life. Her goal is to be as informative as possible about her health and nutrition. Her strong will

and positivity lead her to substantial balance in life.

Lisa wanted to share her story to help other adoptees become more aware of the underlying battles that they may face with adoption. For more information, feel free to contact her at: llnelsonswritingwell@gmail.com.

Elaine Turso, known as "Elaine The Brain," has been a creative, self-made, problem-solving entrepreneur since 2001. As the Chief Visionary Partner for the newly founded INsource It Marketing Agency, Elaine enjoys supporting other entrepreneurs with their businesses, getting shit done for them, so they can focus on their zone of genius.

Her friends call her "Elaine The Brain" because she gets intuitive "Pop Rocks" that help people find creative solutions to their problems. She founded the Get Shit Done Together Group to motivate and encourage her clients to maintain their momentum and achieve their goals.

She also runs her own podcast (The Potty Mouth Pep Talk) where she provides uplifting and motivational pep talks, that sometimes use colorful sentence enhancers. She is also a co-host of the Life by Design, Not Default podcast with her business bestie, K. Paige Engle.

She is a Legacy Leader within Polka Dot Powerhouse, a women's organization she has been a part of since 2016. She is the Managing Director for the Diamond Membership level. She was voted the "One to Watch," with an award in 2017.

She is a mother to Alexis and Anthony, wife to Mike, and dog mom to Paisley, Chloe, and her grandpuppy, Jax. And her favorite things include watching "Friends" re-runs, spiced chai lattes with almond milk, "Mary Poppins," Disneyland, and (of course) profanity.

Angela Witczak lives in the Greatest Place on Earth in Baraboo, WI with her husband, a few of her eight children, and her dog, KW. She is the bestselling author of *Life is a Circus, Enjoy the Show*, and a fundraiser extraordinaire. She lives by the words, "If you find yourself saying someone ought to do something about that, then take a look in the mirror, because you are someone".

Angela sits on a variety of community boards, from the local homeless shelter, to committees that improve and update her local parks. She has raised almost a million dollars for local charities and causes, believing that everyone matters. She doesn't ever sit still unless she is sleeping, and she loves to tell people that she loves them and that they are valuable.

When she is not hanging out at the circus, she spends her days helping individuals and organizations make a difference in their lives, one day at a time. She can be reached at choosetoday366@gmail.com

Keely Crook was born and raised near Madison, Wisconsin. She has an affinity towards reading books that help her better understand herself and the world around her, in addition to reading books on canning, gardening and, most recently, dog training.

When she isn't reading up on a new topic of interest, you can find her hiking the trails or finding peace in the wilderness. She currently lives in Wisconsin.

She hopes that her chapter will inspire other women to believe in themselves and to help them navigate their own way to a happier life.

Abbie Lorine (Born and raised in Southern Illinois) has weathered many storms in her life; from being a teen mom, to living in a domestic violence shelter, and other complex medical situations. At times, these have left her feeling depressed and with no confidence. Through hard work, therapy, and spiritual perseverance, she rose like a phoenix from the ashes.

Now, as an aspiring "mompreneur," her mission is to make sure women feel loved, worthy, and accepted. She enjoys bringing her inspirational work to schools, youth challenges, and podcasts. Living now in Rock Springs, WI, she works to create generational impact alongside her children, Abreanna, Aspynn, Destyni, and Aizik. Abbie is a birth mother to Noah and angel momma to six.

Connect with Abbie at miss.author.abbie@gmail.com

Cindy Strom is an RN, BSN, Certified High Performance Coach, and personal development coach. In each of these roles, she compassionately supports others, with a special interest in aiding caregivers who have a loved one with Alzheimer's or dementia. After her mom was diagnosed with Alzheimer's, she did a deep dive into health, especially proactive brain health. She loves to discuss what she has learned with those curious about health and longevity.

Cindy lives in Madison, WI with her partner, Paul, two cats, and one exceptionally sweet rescue dog. Cindy has previously volunteered as an EMT, wildlife rehabilitation volunteer, and currently volunteers at a local farm sanctuary. During her spare time, Cindy loves being outdoors. Bicycling, hiking, swimming, and snowshoeing are some of her favorite activities. Other interests include travel, camping, and entertaining friends and family.

Laura Hulleman, the creator of the Endotype Formula, is a powerful truth teller. Her superpower is helping people believe that being themselves as they are designed is more than enough. Once a person is grounded in their identity, they can begin to operate from their zone of genius and experience more peace every day.

Laura spent years researching and recognizing the patterns that created the Endotype Formula, the most comprehensive and advanced personality assessment available at this time. Right now, she takes coaches and entrepreneurs on an adventure into their Endotype Formula to improve their businesses, embody their brand identity, and attract their ideal clientele.

She and her two boys live in a tree house in Wisconsin, where they enjoy cozy fires in the winter, and camping, fishing and kayaking all summer long.

Thank you, dear reader, for taking this walk with us. We hope that you learned more about yourself and are inspired by these amazing authors. If we have one goal for you, it is that you move forward in your life ready to do things your way, to be on your own walk.

Although your walk is unique, you do not have to do it alone. One of the antidotes to comparison is connection. Keep walking over to our website to join our community and access the bonus content, videos, and events we have prepared just for YOU.

Remember when the road seems uphill and each step is exhausting, you have a group of women supporting and cheering for you.

Keep doing your walk, your way!
Angela and Laura
www.mywalkmyway.com

The
Journey
Continues
Fall
2022

www.mywalkmyway.com

CPSIA information can be obtained
at www.ICGtesting.com
Printed in the USA
BVHW041617261221
624806BV00010B/250